HERE'S WHAT PEOPLE ARE SAYING ABOUT THIS BOOK!

I have often been saddened by my own lack of sincere passion and my strivings for self-protection. I am very aware that my human experiences have spoken louder than the gospel as it pertains to my understanding of love. Scotty Smith has given us a gift, not only in the poetry of his language, but also in the transparency of his story. Within these pages are words that stir the soul, guiding us on our journeys toward understanding the love of God—a love powerful enough to restore passion in the dark and weathered corners of our lives.

—DAN HASELTINE, Songwriter and Lead Singer of Jars of Clay

Scotty's words flow like those of a man who has had a lifelong search quenched at the ever-deepening fountain of God's love and grace. His words are an irresistible invitation to the soul to come and drink deeply along with him. I'm reminded as I read what a treasure his friendship is because he consistently makes me want to know Jesus better.

—STEVEN CURTIS CHAPMAN, Author, Songwriter, and
   Recording Artist

Although I have never met Scotty Smith, I feel as if I know him after reading the words of his testimony. Objects of His Affection *describes the personal revival that I believe the average church member is desperate to experience. My prayer as you read this book is that your heart might break free from its spiritual twilight zone into the glorious light of God's love.*

—ANNE GRAHAM LOTZ, AnGelMinistries

Objects of His Affection *is a dynamite book. It's not a comfortable book, but then, dynamite hardly ever is. If you use it to blast away the concrete that is often defined as religion and propriety, you're in for a surprise. You'll discover a God who loves what is under the concrete far more than you ever believed. Then you'll be free. Trust me on this: Read this book.*

> —STEVE BROWN, Professor of Preaching, Reformed
> Theological Seminary, Orlando, Florida
> Teacher, *Key Life* radio program

If the unexamined life is not worth living, then it is to Jesus we must go, asking him through his Word to illumine, magnify, and examine us. Scotty Smith has obviously asked Jesus, and he has answered.

> —MICHAEL CARD, Author, Teacher, and Recording Artist

We all need to be reminded that God delights in us and wants us to delight in him. In person, Scotty Smith's gentle spirit and pastor's heart do just that. In this book, his words gracefully reveal not only his own heart, but also the heart of our loving Father.

> —TWILA PARIS, Author, Songwriter, and Recording Artist

Scotty Smith is my pastor and has been for over ten years. I look to him as my pastor because of lines like this from his new book: "I've been such a bound man. I've been a pastor proclaiming freedom for the prisoners while I lay buried under the jail." I am a weak, struggling human in need of so much guidance from God. Thanks, Scotty, for your courage to reveal your humanity in a quick-to-judge world. When our leaders are open and honest about their frailty, it gives courage to us, the sheep.

> —PETER JENKINS, Author of *A Walk across America* and
> *Looking for Alaska*

I didn't count the pages, but anyway you number them, Objects of His Affection *is a big book. Big books enlarge the heart and mind. They work on you from the inside out. They make your eyes leak from all the truth and beauty filling up your insides. This is Scotty Smith's "well done, bravo" book. It's about a wounded healer writing in response to the overwhelming grace of God. Scotty gets very real, and every reader benefits.*

—CHARLIE PEACOCK, Musician and Author of *At the Crossroads*

I've admired Scotty as a brilliant theologian for over a decade, but I never felt I really knew him until reading this book. With aching vulnerability he exposes his desperate need for hope and healing. And his poignant testimony of a little boy's broken heart and the subsequent years of self-protective religiosity is a powerful reminder to trust God with our despair and run to him for refuge. I love this book!

—KIM HILL, Recording Artist

How lucky we are to have a man in this position present himself as he really is, a humble and broken man with a heart that is just now beginning to heal. Instead of trying to portray himself as a great man, his true greatness shines through as he shares his life experience in full color.

—ALISON KRAUS, Songwriter and Recording Artist

With his heart open wide, Scotty Smith shares his pain, shame, and joy in order to help our hearts open wide to the healing, mercy, and beauty of God's grace. Through powerful, personal experiences and deep scriptural insight, Scotty leads those of us whom life has left shattered, callused, or numb into the renewing love and peace of Jesus.

—BRYAN CHAPELL, President, Covenant Theological Seminary

OBJECTS *of* HIS *affection*

OBJECTS
of HIS
affection

COMING ALIVE
TO THE COMPELLING
love OF GOD

HOWARD
PUBLISHING CO.

SCOTTY SMITH
FOREWORD BY DR. DAN ALLENDER

Our purpose at Howard Publishing is to:
- *Increase faith* in the hearts of growing Christians
- *Inspire holiness* in the lives of believers
- *Instill hope* in the hearts of struggling people everywhere

Because He's coming again!

Objects of His Affection © 2001 by Scotty Smith
All rights reserved. Printed in the United States of America

Published by Howard Publishing Co., Inc.
3117 North 7th Street, West Monroe, Louisiana 71291-2227

01 02 03 04 05 06 07 08 09 10   10 9 8 7 6 5 4 3 2

Edited by Philis Boultinghouse
Interior design by Stephanie Denney

Library of Congress Cataloging-in-Publication Data

    Smith, Scotty, 1950–
        Objects of His affection: coming alive to the compelling love of God / Scotty
        Smith.
           p. cm.
        ISBN 1-58229-189-6
         1. Christian life—Meditations. I. Title.

    BV4501.3 .S655 2001
    231'.6—dc21

                                    2001026413

Scripture quotations not otherwise marked are taken from the Holy Bible, New International Version. Copyright © 1973, 1978, 1984 International Bible Society. Used by permission of Zondervan Bible Publishers. Other Scriptures are quoted from the New American Standard Bible (NASB), © 1973 by The Lockman Foundation; and The Message (MSG), © 1994 by Eugene H. Peterson.

TO MOM
*M*ARTHA WARD SMITH
YOUR AMAZING *smile* WILL ALWAYS INVITE ME
TO KNOW THE LOVING AND
JOYFUL *heart* OF GOD

TO DAD
*T*HOMAS ARGO SMITH
THANKS FOR *giving* ME A LOVE FOR ADVENTURE,
YOUR *heart,* AND YOUR TEARS

Contents

OBJECTS *of* HIS *affection*

FOREWORD

A dear friend writes this book. I knew Scotty Smith when I was a young, irreverent seminarian who drifted into the study of theology propelled by the winds of the drug movement, seared by the acrid rage of tear gas, and as empty as the slogans of peace and love. I was thrown into a school that was robust in its academic demands and severe in its call to theological accuracy. Truth was true, knowable, and communicable—and one had better do it right. I was a former member of the SDS (and if you are too young to know what that stands for, think of Simon the Zealot) sitting with older, more mature men who bathed daily, had short hair, and used pot to cook soup. I was out of place. I was in trouble.

I will never forget hearing an intense, cool, older student talking about the Bible in ways that were compelling and honest. His words

were well crafted, but the rhythm of his speech and the call of his heart were marked with a reality, a depth, and a humanity that I may have missed in others but I could not escape in him. I became his friend. I recall wondering if the gospel would ever come to mean as much to me as it did to Scotty.

Little did I know of his life, and even less did the idea of knowing about a human life seem important. What was important was truth. Truth changed the heart and turned the twisted currents of one's past into the peaceful waters of life. I wish someone had told me the truth about truth and about life, but it seemed we were mostly caught up in knowing what to believe, not whether those beliefs really made that much difference in our relationships. Yet there was a hint of something extravagant, generous, and kind about Scotty that prompted intrigue and envy. He lived near the heat of life in ways that attracted and frightened me. I know him well. I know and love his wife, Darlene. I have had the privilege of countless discussions with them about life, theology, the human heart, and the great call of the Kingdom of God. His writing and preaching continue to shape my comprehension of the gospel. However, little of what I have written is why I think this book is compelling.

Scotty is a broken fool. He has been a man caught up in the gospel yet lost in a flight from reality. His story is an odd adventure of how one can be thrilled by the gospel but unaware of God's mad, wild, reckless pursuit of us. How tragic to know God's love and not know the love of God! I confess these words are less a description of Scotty than they are of me. Yet it is this man's courageous journey to face his own cowardice, fragility, and need that pierced my own disbelief and complacency. Kafka said a good book is like an ax blow that shatters the frozen parts of our heart. This is a good book. It is a piercing, inviting, awesome invitation to know what I know but I somehow fail to enjoy—being the object of God's immense, irresistible, incomprehensible passion. I can simply promise—read and you will never be the same again.

Dr. Dan B. Allender
President, Mars Hill Graduate School

ACKNOWLEDGMENTS

There are so many special people who have played a part in helping my selfish, unbelieving heart come alive to the delight of God and his joyful singing over all his children—just as there are so many who have helped me tell his and this story. I deeply appreciate all of you.

To Darlene, my wife. You continue to be a tenacious and faithful warrior of the heart, calling me to places I would never go without your understanding, passion, and God's grace. I love you and look forward to growing old with you.

To my two children, Kristin and Scott, and my son-in-law, Matt. I am so proud of each of you. May we continue to dance together to the healing and liberating music of God's love.

To Ruth Williams Smith, my stepmom. Ruth, words cannot adequately express my gratitude to you for your role in helping me and Dad connect and for helping him give me Mom's story.

To my brother, Moose. Thanks for your love, the gift of music, and for keeping the memory of Mom alive in my soul. Special thanks as well to your wife, Sue, and to your children, Geoff, Susannah, and Isaac. And welcome, Macy! All of you extend the welcoming heart of God so well.

To Philis Boultinghouse, my editor, and the Howard Publishing family. Thanks for the gracious gift of helping me tell and craft these stories of God's amazing love as friends and not as a company.

To Sue McCallum, my assistant. For who you are and the many ways you serve me so faithfully, I praise God.

To Virginia Bousquet, Nancy Puryear, Katie Haseltine, and Jana Brown. Thanks to each of you for investing your heart, time, and your love for God's people in creating discussion questions calculated to make us redemptively squirm and run to the God of all grace.

To Gary and Gale Kennedy, Phoebe and Marvin Nischan, Wayne and Pat Dunn, and Walter and Anita Oglive. Your generous gifts of hospitality refresh this weary journeyman more than you realize.

To Peter and Rita Jenkins. Thanks for opening Alaska and your hearts to Scott and me. The timing and tenor of our visit was so of God.

To Rose Marie Miller, my spiritual mom. Keep praying! Keep driving me to Jesus and his grace. I miss Jack so much.

To Phil Cherico. You are a reminder to me that God continues to give good gifts to those who wait.

To Dan Allender, Scott Roley, and Mike Card. You know.

To Buddy Greene, Parke Brown, John Patton, and Steven Curtis. You guys are a primary means of grace, hope, and encouragement in my life. I love you.

To Lloyd Shadrach and Jeff Schulte. You washed my feet and heart during a dark time. I will never forget.

To Ma and Pa Compton. Thanks for always saying and for meaning, "Son, we love you and are so proud of you."

To my Small Group: Bruce and Debbie McCurdy, Geoff and Jan Moore, Arlin and Kathy Troyer, and Mike and Jeannie Malloy. A community of brokenness is a garden of faith, hope, and love.

To the whole Christ Community family. Thanks for not trading me in for a Diet Coke.

And finally, thanks to many other friends who will forgive me when I remember you and feel shame and guilt for not including your name!

Game Boy in Paradise

Dear Dad,

It seems a bit strange to open this book with a letter to you. But as I have been writing over the last year, my words feel more and more like a correspondence between hearts—yours and mine. Having signed a contract to write for new friends, I had no idea at the time what I had *really* signed on for. Though I started out with a commitment to put into written form some of the things I have been learning about the love of God, the God of love had a different agenda in mind. Dad, a big part of *his* plan involved you and me—our relationship.

How can I express my joy for what has only recently been happening between us? You are eighty-one and I am fifty, and we are becoming friends. Two guys who have struggled with relationships all our lives are finally connecting with each other in a way we've

both longed for. A father and son who have only lived side by side are tasting a little face-to-face relationship. And Dad, I am hungry for more.

For all the ways I've made it difficult for us to get close until now, I am sorry. Please forgive me. It's hard not to be weighted down with the anchor of old regrets and the fruitless world of fresh "if only's." Let's make the best use of the time we have left.

Stewards together of a life-shaping tragedy, we did the best we could. At best, we became survivors. I was eleven and you were forty-two. But now, we can finally talk about it. As you said, "The life went out of all of us on that day." It's true. It really did. But now, that which tore us apart is bringing us together. The wound is becoming the healer.

In the Bible, fifty is an important number. Every fifty years Israel was to celebrate a year of Jubilee—a year in which debts would be cancelled and prisoners set free. It was to be a yearlong celebration of mercy, grace, and freedom. I have been a bound man for most of my fifty years, even as the debt to love well has continued to mount. Thanks for helping loose some of my chains.

So, Dad, this book has emerged out of many stories, not the least of which is ours. In it, I tell the story of God's love. You and I have never talked a whole lot about eternal things with each other, but I hope these words and stories will enable us to dialogue some about God, his world, and the way he pursues us for rich relationship.

This past summer, Scott and I were invited by some good friends up to Seward, Alaska, to fish for salmon and halibut in Resurrection Bay. It was incredible! Not only did we bring back fifty pounds of the filet of glory, but the whole time we shamelessly acted like two little boys in a candy shop.

One of the most lasting impressions of our trip, a memory I want to hold on to the rest of my days in this world, occurred on our train ride from Seward to Anchorage—the day we left to catch our flight back to Nashville. For three hours Scott and I fought for the camera as we ran back and forth on both sides of our panoramic train car trying to capture on film the display of glory before our eyes. You've been there—you know what I'm talking about. Anyway, right in the middle of all of our grandiose oohing and aahing, I looked down and almost tripped over a young boy, I'd say about ten or so, sitting on the floor playing with a hand-held computer game. On one of the most beautiful days in the history of the world, right in the midst of so much mind-boggling splendor, and he was playing Game Boy!

He was oblivious to it all—totally absorbed in his little game. I wanted to rip the expensive toy out of his hands and say, "Wake up! What are you doing? Look all around you. How can you settle for Game Boy while riding through paradise?" But his mom was sitting next to him reading her fashion magazine, so I decided to mind my own business and keep fighting with Scott for our camera.

I came away from that train ride thinking a whole lot about God and his love. Dad, there is no greater adventure I've even attempted than exposing my heart to the wild affections of God. And yet I've had to realize how much we're all like that young boy on the train. We get absorbed and content in our own various and sundry games while God bombards us with opportunities to discover the wonders

of his love. And the amazing thing is, God is pursuing us with passion and delight. He actually enjoys us!

Trying to get God's love from my head to my heart has been a lifetime struggle. I think you'll relate as you read, because so many of my stories involve stuff we've been through together.

I've been able to make a little sense of all the unconscionable suffering in the world as I've taken the necessary time to reflect on Jesus' death on the cross. It's been the suffering Jesus who has kept me from despair and cynicism. And strangely enough, Dad, I'm finding more freedom to love other people only as I spend more time grieving my losses—make that our losses. Go figure! God's love is as paradoxical as it is freeing.

I love you and look forward to being with you soon.

Love,
Scotty

THE LORD DID NOT SET HIS *affection* ON YOU
AND CHOOSE YOU BECAUSE YOU WERE MORE
NUMEROUS THAN OTHER PEOPLES.
FOR YOU WERE THE FEWEST OF ALL PEOPLE.
BUT IT WAS BECAUSE THE LORD *loved* YOU.
—DEUTERONOMY 7:7–8

Thy *mercy,* my God, is the theme of my song,
The joy of my *heart,* and the boast of my tongue.
Thy free *grace,* alone from the first to the last,
Hath won my *affection* and bound my soul fast.

Thy *mercy* is more than a match for my heart,
Which *wonders* to feel its own hardness depart.
Dissolved by Thy *goodness,* I fall to the ground
And weep to the *praise* of the mercy I've found.

*J*ohn Stocker (1777)

Coming Alive to the Love of God

This book is a study and story of the heart's journey in coming alive to the compelling love of God. The chapters that follow wrestle with many of the difficulties and delights of knowing "this love that surpasses knowledge" (Ephesians 3:19). It is very much a work in process, for I am a fellow traveler. I do not pretend to have written a systematic study of the love of God; rather, I write out of my own longing for greater joy and freedom in God's love. I write with more desire than expertise, with more brokenness than togetherness.

Throughout this study, we'll come again and again to a passage in Zephaniah that shocks our sensibilities and fills our hearts with longing:

Sing, O Daughter of Zion;
    shout aloud, O Israel!
Be glad and rejoice with all your heart,

O Daughter of Jerusalem!
The LORD has taken away your punishment,
 he has turned back your enemy.
The LORD, the King of Israel, is with you;
 never again will you fear any harm.
On that day they will say to Jerusalem,
 "Do not fear, O Zion;
 do not let your hands hang limp.
The LORD your God is with you,
 he is mighty to save.
He will take great delight in you,
 he will quiet you with his love,
 he will rejoice over you with singing." (Zephaniah 3:14–17)

The promises of this incredible passage of scripture are unparalleled. But before we can savor the glory of God's promises, we must first taste the paradox in Zephaniah's magnificent announcement. Prior to this amazing expression of love, God's prophet Zephaniah had blasted the Israelite people for their disobedience.

I will stretch out my hand against Judah
 and against all who live in Jerusalem....
At that time I will search Jerusalem with lamps
 and punish those who are complacent,
 who are like wine left on its dregs,
who think, "The LORD will do nothing,
 either good or bad."
Their wealth will be plundered,
 their houses demolished.
They will build houses
 but not live in them;
they will plant vineyards
 but not drink the wine. (Zephaniah 1:4, 12–13)

To take hold of the communitarian love and joy of the Godhead is one thing. To accept God's painful assessment of our hearts is another. As in Zephaniah's day, so in ours: Very few of us really believe that we deserve God's punishment. Many of us actually feel he owes us an apology or two.

OUR DESPERATE NEED

We've become acclimated to a condition we should never have gotten used to: a stagnant pool of religious forms and sentimentality along with buckets full of cultural legalisms. Inoculated with enough "god-speak" to immunize our consciences, we can't hear the thunderous river of God's grace roaring invitingly in the Bibles we read and the hymns we sing—a grace that beckons us to enter, be washed, and set free. Let's face it, apart from God's Spirit mightily at work in our hearts, we're morons!

Either out of ignorance or unbelief or quite possibly both, we simply have precious little firsthand experience with the magnitude of our Father's love for his people. And some of us are simply not concerned about the whole matter because we've been seduced and dulled by affairs of the heart.

But lacking awareness of our need does not diminish its intensity. We *desperately* need to have the eyes of our hearts opened to the magnitude of God's love revealed in Jesus Christ.

Please don't get the idea that this book will help you enter a state of spiritual bliss and carry you above the struggles of everyday life. To the contrary, God's love takes us into the chaos of a broken world

and messy relationships rather than providing a way of superspiritual escape. Only the gospel of God's grace can keep us from despair.

SOJOURNING TOGETHER

Are *you* ready for the journey? Indeed, how do our hearts come alive to the compelling love of God? I suggest the following elements:

Spirit. Only the Holy Spirit can reveal both our needs and the supply of God's love to meet our needs. Conviction is a work of the Spirit, and love is a fruit of the Spirit (Galatians 5:22). In fact, it is the Spirit's work to inundate our hearts with God's love for us: "And hope does not disappoint us, because God has poured out his love into our hearts by the Holy Spirit, whom he has given us" (Romans 5:5). In this verse, Paul chose the same word used in Acts 2:17 to describe the outpouring of the Holy Spirit on the Day of Pentecost. The Holy Spirit is not begrudging in making known the immensity of God's love. Ask God's Holy Spirit to be at work in your heart as you read; you might even ask a few other friends in Christ to pray for you in the coming weeks. You may want to consider reading the book with a few of your friends or in your small group, utilizing the discussion questions included in the back of the book.

Scripture. Let us together give ourselves to the study of and reflection on the Scriptures. To know the love of God, we must seek the God of love's instruction. The Bible is his book, revealing what he wants us to know about all things. Treat his words with far more respect than mine.

Story. This book contains many stories—stories from my own life as well as stories from the lives of others whom I've met along my journey. It hasn't been easy to be vulnerable regarding my weaknesses and failures in love. Writing this book has felt as if the zip file of my heart has been decompressed and turned loose before the face of God and many friends. I have never hurt so badly, nor have I ever felt so close to the Lord. Having just turned fifty, little did I realize that my Jubilee year would prove to be so intense; but freedom for the heart is not easily won. Jesus has come to set prisoners free, and I have had to confront the depth and the many forms of my own imprisonment. But if the Son sets you free, you are free indeed!

My purpose in the use of storytelling is twofold: First, I pray it will help you uncover the hidden stories of your life. Often, it is as we remember our stories—painful as well as happy stories—that we discover our need for forgiveness, freedom, and healing. Second, I pray you will learn to access your own story in the context of God's Story. Each of us is a part of a larger narrative that God is writing. Perhaps you and those friends I earlier recommended you read this book with can learn how to share your stories with one another as well.

Silence. The hardest work this journey will require is making time for stillness. You can read this book in a few hours, but to reflect, journal, meditate, pray, and experience the quieting love of God will take time and quiet.

Each chapter concludes with a prayer written to guide you in meditating upon and applying its main themes to your heart and life. I suggest you use these prayers to lead you into adoration and action.

Surrender. As you read, you quite probably will experience

profound moments as God begins to show you the height, depth, width, and breadth of his love for you in Jesus. God is committed to removing the obstacles in our hearts that keep us from loving well. We must be committed to surrendering our all to his love. We are to love as he loves us.

In essence, this is the story of God's pursuing and passionate mercy revealed in his Word and through his Son. It is the story of how subjects of futility and foolishness become objects of God's affection. It's about how God makes worshipers out of idolaters, a wife out of a whore.

Wherever you find yourself in life, your loving Father is in hot pursuit of you. Open wide your heart. Dive into the depths of his love. Rest in his gentle embrace. Hear his invitation:

Come, ye thirsty, come, and welcome,
God's free bounty glorify;
True belief and true repentance,
Ev'ry grace that brings you nigh.

Let not conscience make you linger,
Nor of fitness fondly dream;
All the fitness he requireth
Is to feel your need of him.

Come, ye weary, heavy-laden,
Lost and ruined by the fall;
If you tarry till you're better,
You will never come at all.

Lo! The incarnate God ascended,
Pleads the merit of his blood;
Venture on him, venture wholly;
Let no other trust intrude.

I will arise and go to Jesus,
He will embrace me in his arms;
In the arms of my dear Savior,
O there are ten thousand charms.[1]

But the *Lord* God called to the man,
"Where are you?"
He answered,
"I HEARD you in the garden,
and I was *afraid* because I was naked—so I hid."
—Genesis 3:9–10

O to *grace* how great a debtor
Daily I'm constrained to be!
Let Thy *goodness* like a fettor
Bind my wand'ring *heart* to Thee;
Prone to wander, Lord I feel it,
Prone to leave the God I *love;*
Here's my *heart*, O take and seal it,
Seal it for Thy courts above.

*R*obert Robinson (1735–1790)

CHAPTER ONE

The Restlessness Begins

C an you tell me where Martha Amanda Ward Smith is buried?"
Had I ever spoken her whole name out loud?

"Who?"

"She's my mother; she was buried here in 1961. Martha Ward
Smith." The attendant came back with a map on which he'd circled
her grave and marked it with a yellow highlighter. I walked to the car
feeling as if I'd just come from AAA with a map to a distant destina-
tion. How tacky: a map to my mother's grave. My eyes were already
damp, my heart pregnant with embarrassment and anticipation.

Within two minutes, our car arrived at the designated spot. My
wife, Darlene, and I walked to her grave. With my arm around
Darlene, I looked down at the matured green grass. I eyed the dates
of the marker: September 10, 1923–October 10, 1961. What a
short life—barely thirty-eight years. Stunned by the math, I said,

"Honey, she's been dead longer than she lived." By then, I was leaning on Darlene, my knees buckling beneath me. This was the first time I'd been to Mom's grave since the day we buried her.

My mind drifted back to a day thirty-nine years ago. It had been a crisp, fall day in Graham, North Carolina. I rode my bike home from school as fast as I could with the hope of catching some big bream or maybe a bass or two out of Johnson's Pond about a half a mile from our home. I remember thinking it strange that my mother's car wasn't in the driveway. But it was Friday—the day Mom usually got her hair done in Greensboro—so I figured that maybe she'd stayed a little longer to visit friends. With a handful of cookies and a milk mustache, I grabbed my Zebco 33 Spinner and made a dash for my favorite fishing hole.

Within twenty minutes my rod bent double under the weight of some hungry aquatic creature. It felt huge! With my heart pumping, I had visions of a ten-pound bass, while simply hoping it wasn't one of those ugly snapping turtles that had taken up residence in our neighborhood pond.

After a hearty struggle, my afternoon catch relented and surfaced. I had caught the biggest catfish of my life. I didn't even know there were catfish in Johnson's Pond. Escaping harm from my whiskered friend's barbs, I unhooked him and ran a stick through his gills so I could take him home and show the spoils of my afternoon adventure to Mom.

But as I got closer to the house with my rod in one hand and my slimy, big fish in the other, I could see that Mom's 1960 white Rambler American still wasn't in the driveway. Out of the corner of my eye I saw Mrs. Peters walking across her yard into ours. She was our pastor's wife, and the church's manse was just across the street from us. She didn't look her normal cheerful self.

"Scotty, something bad has happened today."

Immediately—I don't know why—I asked, "Is it Mom? Is she OK?"

"No, Scotty, she's not. Your mother was killed in a car wreck late this morning as she was driving home from Greensboro. I am so sorry. Why don't you come on home with me?"

How does an eleven-year-old absorb such news? I remember the feeling of shock. I couldn't cry. I didn't want to ask questions. I just went numb.

Before long, my only sibling, Moose (legally Steve, but nick-named after the Archie's comic-book character since the eighth grade), came to the Peters' home after junior varsity football practice. Though as close as sixth grade and ninth grade brothers can be, we just kind of looked at each other. No tears, no words; we just sat there in silent aloneness.

The sun went down, and Mrs. Peters made us supper while we waited for our dad to get home. As we sat at the kitchen table, the screen door opened and in walked Pop. "Boys, do you know what has happened?"

We nodded yes. And then he walked right by us into his own paralyzing grief. We never touched, we never talked, we never teared—at least, not together. Never.

To this day I have no idea what happened to my fish or to my Zebco 33 Spinner—but I do know what happened to my heart. That

cool fall day, late in October 1961, represents the beginning of a journey the three of us took into denial, isolation, and survival. Nothing shaped each of us relationally more than the day Mom died. Nothing.

Loud Nonsense

Reverend Peters tried his best to pastor me through the process. I wasn't a Christian at the time, so his religious words offered little more than sentimental and superstitious comfort to me. "Scotty, your mother is in a better place. I know it's hard, so hard. We will gather at the funeral home and…"

As soon as he said the words "funeral home," I got rigid. Nothing and no one could make me go to that eerie facility with people I didn't want to be around to see my mother lying in a satin-lined box with her eyes closed. I simply refused to go to the funeral home—not even once.

> TO THIS DAY I HAVE NO IDEA WHAT HAPPENED TO MY FISH OR TO MY ZEBCO 33 SPINNER— BUT I DO KNOW WHAT HAPPENED TO MY HEART.

As we climbed into the black limousine on the day of the funeral, I wanted to disappear. I wanted to be anywhere other than sitting on the front row of my own mother's funeral service, but I had no choice. I can remember repeating to myself, "Don't look at the casket. Don't look at the casket."

It felt so awful to be stared at and pitied by all those people as we walked into the church. I sat down, set my gaze on the floor, rocked my feet, and filled my mind with loud nonsense. Anything to survive the moment, anything to drown out the sounds and deny the sight of death.

When you are eleven and pushing early adolescence, crying is just about the most uncool thing in the world. When you are eleven and your mom is dead, crying is what you need to do most.

I remember nothing about the service except the color red, the bright red of the carpet that covered the floor of our stately old sanctuary. Another limo ride—this time to the cemetery. I dreaded this more than the funeral itself. From that day on, I have hated and avoided all good-byes. Sitting pensively in my designated graveside chair, I simply "went somewhere else" during the burial service, defiantly ignoring the canvas-covered pile of dirt that would soon be shoveled upon my mom's lifeless body. I tried my best to detach from the proceedings until I made it home and got out of those dreadful, uncomfortable "church clothes." At home, I immediately shifted to another form of detachment: I busied myself with something. With what, I couldn't tell you. It doesn't really matter.

As the day of the funeral came to a reprieveless end, each of us simply went to bed—not to sleep, but to bed. Once again, no talk, no touch, no tears were shared between us. I remember hearing the wails of my father and being afraid.

From that day on, all three of us stayed busy, and we became increasingly restless. For the next thirty-nine years, Dad and I would not have a single conversation about Mom. Not one.

I share with you, dear reader, the journey of my restless heart because I know that you, too—if not consumed with restlessness to the degree I was—hold restlessness in certain chambers of your heart.

SPIRITUAL VENEER

Eight years after Mom's death, the phone rang. "Scotty, are you sitting down? I hate to be the one to tell you, but Debbie is dead. She rolled her Austin Healey going back to school last night. One of her friends also died in the wreck, and another is hurt really bad. Her folks want to know if you will be a pallbearer for the funeral."

All the dark feelings of Mom's death came rushing right back in, even though they hadn't gone very far away. Another car wreck. Someone else ripped out of my life to whom I had given a large part of my heart. Debbie was more a girl friend than a girlfriend, if you know what I mean. And really, that made the loss all the greater. Though we dated all through high school, marriage would not have been in our future, but a lifelong friendship, yes. I didn't have a closer friend in the world. Our kisses were more practice than romantic.

"Uh, uh, I don't know. I'll have to check my schedule." Check my schedule? Check my *schedule?* Since when does anyone check his schedule to determine whether or not to be a pallbearer at his best friend's funeral? I visited her parents one time at their home, but just as with my mom, I refused to go to the funeral home to see Debbie's body. And, much to my shame, I lied, making up some lame excuse about a college exam and bailed out on being a pallbearer or even attending her funeral. To this day, I don't even know where Debbie is buried.

Two people had been torn from my life through untimely deaths. (What is a timely death, anyway?) I was quickly developing the relational skills of a lizard or a desert monk. Having never even begun to process my mom's death and its effect on me, I had no clue what to do with Debbie's. Though I became a Christian a year before Debbie died, my early years in the Lord were all about acquiring biblical information, instruction on the duties of the Christian life, and learning how to defend the faith against late sixties' atheists and agnostics.

A wall of self-protection, a commitment to controlling my world, and a lifestyle of staying busy took over. For the next season of life, theological knowledge and ministry became a substitute for learning how to relate to people and to love well. But how long can such a veneer of spiritual respectability supplant the very reason for which the knowledge of God has been given? Apparently, I wasn't ready to face the truth of me quite yet.

> I WAS QUICKLY DEVELOPING THE RELATIONAL SKILLS OF A LIZARD.

A Noisy Heart

"Two things define you more than the love of God: your busy, noisy heart and the fact that you have yet to deal with your mom's death." Dr. Dan Allender offered these words as an invitation—not as an indictment—in the context of a counseling training seminar in January 1983. Three of my buddies who are involved in vocational ministry and I invested a week with Dan, seeking to sharpen our skills as listeners and caregivers.

A woman from the local community had volunteered to be Dan's counselee each evening and allow us "trainees" to watch the sessions through a mirrored window. The plan was to watch Dan counsel and then process the session together over coffee, after the

counselee was dismissed. When it became obvious the first night that she wasn't going to show up, Dan asked, "Any one of you guys want to take her place?" Impulsively, my hand shot straight up. "Yeah, I'll go for it."

Dan and I had met at Westminster Theological Seminary in 1975 as fellow students. I admired his work and personality and didn't sense I had anything to fear from one I considered a friend. Boy, was I wrong! Only later did one of my three friends confide to me that no sooner had Dan and I entered the observation counseling room than they looked at one another and agreed, "Scotty's going down!"

The truth is, I wish I had "gone down." If I hadn't believed in a prophetic gift before, that day should have been enough to convince me. Dan saw right into the core of my heart, and he gave me the perfect opportunity to submit to the pursuing heart of God. Instead I deflected the opportunity and simply congratulated him on his incredible talents as a counselor. He was neither flattered nor impressed. Though the whole week proved to be a pivotal time for each of us, I will never forget the taste of sadness that I felt from Dan as we drove to the airport. He had watched me squirm and engage in verbal gymnastics the whole week in a vain attempt to deny the profound restlessness in my heart.

How many times had I quoted St. Augustine through the years: "Our hearts are restless until they find rest in Thee." And how often had I thought of Augustine's words as only applicable to the heart of a nonbeliever? Yet restlessness has pretty well defined my inner life. How ironic that the very setting in which I became a Christian in March

1968 was at a showing of the Billy Graham movie *The Restless Ones*. I have been such a bound man—I've been a pastor proclaiming freedom for the prisoners while I lay buried under the jail.

GOD, CLOSING IN

I could hide behind my respectability only so long. My resources, self-sufficiency, and survival skills finally began to fail me. God was closing in. So in March 2000, I sat with my two friends, Scott and Mike, in Franklin, Tennessee, and the floodgates of my heart finally burst open.

> I HAVE BEEN SUCH A BOUND MAN— I'VE BEEN A PASTOR PROCLAIMING FREEDOM FOR THE PRISONERS WHILE I LAY BURIED UNDER THE JAIL.

"Guys, I haven't been to my mother's grave in the thirty-nine years since she's been dead." The words just jumped out there with absolutely no premeditation. I could hardly believe what I was saying. I felt incredulous—exposed, naked, and very ashamed. Immediately I started sobbing. I cried tears that had aged like fine wine deep in the cellar of my soul. I couldn't stop. I didn't want to.

The Holy Spirit chose this moment to throw open the mile-thick curtain behind which I had been hiding for nearly forty years. Dorothy threw open the curtain, revealing the bumbling "wizard" of Oz. Overwhelmingly vulnerable, nevertheless, I began to feel an emerging sense of relief. Scott began to weep, and he and Mike came around me, knelt down, and simply put their hands on me. For a moment I wanted to recoil out of embarrassment, but my two

friends were giving me permission to begin a process I had been running from for way too long. I don't remember how long we were together. Thank heavens, not too many words were offered.

As we sat in Scott's office, I was exhausted by my own tears and still shaking in the aftershock of so much emotion. Yet I felt…well, peaceful, or at least a little bit so.

Some fugitives actually long to be caught, some addicts want desperately to get busted, and some Christians, especially Christian leaders, crave to be freed from the disparity between their words and their hearts. Maybe this is what the prodigal son felt in the far country when he finally came to his senses and started his journey back to his father's house.

> SOME FUGITIVES ACTUALLY LONG TO BE CAUGHT, SOME ADDICTS WANT DESPERATELY TO GET BUSTED, AND SOME CHRISTIANS, ESPECIALLY CHRISTIAN LEADERS, CRAVE TO BE FREED FROM THE DISPARITY BETWEEN THEIR WORDS AND THEIR HEARTS.

After somewhat gathering myself, I called Darlene from my cell phone as I began the drive home from Scott's office. "Honey, we've got to talk when I get there. I hope you're not planning on going anywhere for a while. My time with Mike and Scott undid me. It was really emotional, much more than I expected."

She had been glad the three of us had finally decided to start talking about the strain in our relationship with each other. The three of us had been walking together for twenty years; we had shared so much life together, yet a significant disconnection had grown up between us in the previous couple of years. The purpose of our meeting was to find out why. Neither Darlene nor I could have anticipated the intensity of that visit.

As I pulled into our driveway and then walked in the back door, more feelings of incredulity swept over me. Darlene kissed and hugged me, and then I told her about the afternoon. "Honey, I feel so stupid, like such a coward. I thought we were simply going to talk about friendship and our junk, and then all of a sudden I tell them I had never visited Mom's grave since she died. I've driven by that cemetery dozens of times and have never stopped, not even once. What's with that? Why do you suppose it was with Mike and Scott that such a thing came out?"

Her gift of mercy took the edge off my self-contempt. It was as though Darlene had been waiting for this day, for this moment. She put her arms around me and held me without trying to rescue me. She spoke simple words without any attempt to fix me. "Scotty, I am so sorry. That must have been devastating. I love you and am proud of you." Her touch felt like an invitation to explore my feelings more. Shame began to give way to stirring and stirring to hope.

Far more than Mike and Scott, Darlene had lived with the painful effects of my secret throughout our marriage—the detachment, the busyness, the withdrawal, the passivity, and the fear—along with the arrogant, wordy spirituality. I deserved her anger for the many ways I had loved her so poorly, but she gave me her embrace. The heart of my wife of nearly twenty-eight years longed for her husband to be set free. In that moment, the God of all grace showed up. That moment with Darlene has become for me a concrete and treasured expression of God's love.

SHAME BEGAN TO
GIVE WAY TO
STIRRING AND
STIRRING TO HOPE.

It was then that my noisy heart took its first wobbly step away from the restlessness that had plagued me all those thirty-nine years. Though at the time of this writing it's only been a brief nine months since my "day of revelation" with my two friends, my heart continues to come more and more alive to the compelling love of God with each passing day. My realization of his love and the joy that is imbedded in relationship with him has plunged me into a swiftly flowing river that brings me closer and closer to his heart.

*D*ear God of Grace and Mercy,

Please help me sort though my emotions. Like Scotty, I, too, have wounds, hurts, and disappointments that at times have more power over my heart than does your love. I need to know that you will not despise me in my weakness or reject me for my foolishness.

I confess—I am afraid of getting stuck in the past. Isn't it best just to leave some things alone? God, shouldn't we just move ahead in life and try harder to be good? I do not want to live my life as a prisoner to victimization. But my own prayer mocks me; for I see in the eyes of those I love a reflection of a prisoner. Lord, I love so haphazardly, so selectively, so poorly.

Please give me courage to face the pain of my story honestly and to identify the matters of my heart. And please give me a hope that will enable me to enter the freedom you have promised through your Son. And God, please lead me to some of your children who can help me in this journey. In the name of Jesus, amen.

THE LORD HAS TAKEN AWAY YOUR PUNISHMENT,
HE HAS TURNED BACK YOUR ENEMY....
THE LORD, YOUR GOD IS WITH YOU,
HE IS *mighty* TO SAVE.
HE WILL TAKE GREAT DELIGHT IN YOU,
HE WILL QUIET YOU WITH HIS *love*,
HE WILL REJOICE OVER YOU WITH SINGING.
—ZEPHANIAH 3:15, 17

And can it be that I should *gain*
An interest in the *Savior's* blood?
Died He for me, who caused His pain?
For me, who Him to death pursued?
Amazing love! How can it be
That Thou, my God, shouldst die for me?

*C*harles Wesley (1707–1788)

CHAPTER TWO

God's Great Delight

Blindfolded with one of my own red jogging bandannas, I ducked my head down and scrunched into the backseat of the car. Really, I had no idea where this little escapade would take us. Though dense, I'm not stupid. I had figured Darlene would plan something, but I am a pretty difficult guy to surprise. In fact, I have worked hard most of my life not to be surprised about anything or anyone. Life seems to go easier that way. Most of my surprises have been calls, visits, and letters I had just as soon never received!

Being one who has no sense of direction, even without a blindfold, try as I might, I could not even begin to tell which direction we were going. *This sounds like Green Hills traffic,* I thought. *Maybe we're going to Mario's. Veal Parmengiana and cheesecake, here I come! That's why she made me change out of my UNC hat and jeans.*

Wait a minute. We would have been at Mario's by now. Seems like

we've been driving for about twenty minutes, and we've made several turns. I know, we're going to Peacock Hill Country Inn for the night, my favorite bed-and-breakfast. She's already got our stuff there. We'll have a candlelight dinner, hot tub for a while, and…way to go, Darlene. You're awesome!

The guessing game was over as Darlene chimed in with the obvious joy of anticipation, "We're here. Just sit still, Scotty. I'll come around and get you." Opening my door as though she was transporting royalty, Darlene took me by the hand, and we walked what seemed to be about twenty-five yards.

"OK, watch your step now." Nothing but the song of a few birds and the unfamiliar sound of a creaking door gave me any sense of context. And then, "Surprise!" Darlene lifted my blindfold as I made my way into a room full of colorful decorations and tables of food and drink. Fifty or so friends spontaneously erupted into that age-old (or is that old-age) classic, "Happy birthday to yoou. Happy birthday to yoouuu.…"

It was that historic and dreaded-by-most, fortieth birthday party. You know, the one that is usually accompanied by black decorations and silly slogans like, "Lordy, Lordy, Scotty's forty" or "Welcome to the over-the-hill gang." Such parties are complete with cups, hats, cards, and gifts—all aimed at welcoming you into the land of AARP and impending senility.

"Haappy birrrthdaaaay.…" I started singing along with my friends, singing my own birthday song! Though very comfortable standing before a large group as a speaker, getting this kind of attention made me feel awkward and a little embarrassed. How can a song that takes thirty seconds to sing seem like it's taking an hour? They, make that *we*, continued, "deaarrrr Scoooootttyyyyy...." Squirming, careful not to make much eye contact, ready for this little ditty of a song to be over..."Haappyyy birrrrrthdayyyyyy tooooo youuuuuuu." More applause, whistles, cheers, and I was beet red and ready to move out of the focus of all eyes and into the crowd as one among many.

Rewind, my brother's party band, filled the room with the sounds of my youth, as they broke into the national anthem of what we from the Carolinas call "beach music": "Sugar Pie Honey Bunch, you know that I love you. I can't help myself. I love you and nobody else." Hugs and happiness, my friends lined up to genuinely welcome me—thrilled to see that they had actually surprised me for a change.

Dancing and feasting on tons of tasty eats continued. Everyone really seemed to be glad—not just because of the great party Darlene had pulled off, but glad for me, "dear Scotty."

AWKWARD OBJECTS OF AFFECTION

It would be another ten years before I would come to the pivotal encounter I described in chapter one. At age forty, I was still very much filled with the restlessness that kept God at a distance. This restlessness not only affected my relationship with the Lover of my soul; it also distanced me from people who loved and cared for me.

Though it felt good to be the reason for the gathering and the object of so much attention, I was uncomfortable with all the adoration. It's hard to sit still and sustain the intensity of eyes, smiles, and

affirmation. There's an awkwardness that comes with an intentional gaze of regard. There is a worrisome suspicion that if people, including my best friends, *really* knew me—if they were aware of all the junk, weakness, fears, and inconsistencies of my life—they wouldn't be quite so glad to see me coming. Do you relate?

We sometimes feel awkward as the "object of someone's affection." We find ways to deflect the praise and attention of others by turning the praise back on them or by changing the conversation to a safer, impersonal topic. We minimize compliments ("Aw shucks; it really wasn't anything."), we turn the focus back on the giver ("That's nothing compared to what you do!"), or we spiritualize the attention ("It wasn't really me; it was the Lord."). Isn't this how we're supposed to respond? Isn't this what the Bible calls humility? Or maybe it's just natural shyness. Some see such exaggerated "humility" as "low self-esteem."

> WHAT WOULD IT FEEL LIKE IN YOUR HEART TO KNOW THAT GOD NOT ONLY *ACCEPTS* YOU BUT THAT HE ALSO RICHLY *ENJOYS* YOU?

The truth is, we all long to be appreciated and enjoyed by the people in our worlds. If Darlene *hadn't* done something special for my fortieth birthday, I would have sulked around for a couple of weeks in a frowny-faced funk—kind of like Eeyore, the forlorn donkey in the Winnie the Pooh tales.

We yearn for the attention and appreciation of others, yet we run from it when it's given. It's like being in two states of mind simultaneously. When people come too close, we pull back. When people stay away, we feel lonely and sad. Does this sound at all familiar to you? Am I the only mess around here?

As Christians, how are we to understand such relational turbulence and ambivalence? Are we to become stoics, cauterizing emotion so we become immune to praise and rejection? Or maybe we simply need a better self-image so we can move into our world with confidence and a well-developed "self-love."

No, our heavenly Father isn't calling us to kill all desire and hope of enjoyment and being enjoyed. Neither does he instruct us to work hard to overcome a bad self-image. Rather, he calls us to develop a "delightful" relationship with him and then to base all other relationships on this most holy relationship of all.

DARE WE ACCEPT GOD'S DELIGHT?

What would it feel like in your heart to know that God not only *accepts* you but that he also richly *enjoys* you? To know that your company is his pleasure, your fellowship his joy, your face his delight? What effect would such a viewpoint have on how you think about God, yourself, and others? How would that belief shape your view of *all* things—even how you chart the whole course of your life?

Right in the middle of what has been called the John 3:16 of the Old Testament, the promise of God's delight in us gushes forth like an artesian well in the Sahara desert:

> The LORD your God is with you,
>   he is mighty to save.
> He will take great delight in you,
>   he will quiet you with his love,
>   he will rejoice over you with singing. (Zephaniah 3:17)

Astonishing, isn't it? Zephaniah states that God is not only *with* us through his mighty salvation but that he, quintessentially, is the Great Delighter and that his great delight is found in *us!* And as if that weren't enough, Zephaniah goes on to say that God is tender toward us and will *quiet* our fears and worries with his love and that in his great delight, he rejoices over us with *singing!*

For many of us, believing that God is actually a God of intense delight is a huge step of progress in our faith. Many of us have never dared to see this side of God; we've focused only on his judgment and his wrath. But the truth is, God really likes being God! In his presence is the fullness of joy.

KNOWING GOD AS OUR DELIGHT

Not only does God delight in us, but we are called to delight in him. King David decrees, "Delight yourself in the LORD and he will give you the desires of your heart" (Psalm 37:4). God himself is to be delighted in—not simply for what he does and gives—but for who he is. The shepherd-king speaks of a vital relationship between our delight and the desires of our hearts.

> GOD REALLY LIKES BEING GOD! IN HIS PRESENCE IS THE FULLNESS OF JOY.

To know God as our delight is to unlock and fulfill the mystery of our hearts' desires. What a magnificent invitation! What a sobering warning!

God calls his people—his beloved "Daughter" (Zephaniah 3:14)—to respond to his devotion with measureless gladness. O. Palmer Robertson, author and scholar, expounds on God's command that his people be joyful: "Not with limpid and fainting spirits, but with all your heart you must rejoice. Cast aside all cautious reserve. Let down your guard against the possibility of future disappointment. Shout aloud! Sing! Be jubilant!"[1] Indeed, we can delight ourselves in the Lord only because and truly because God greatly delights in us!

TOO GOOD TO BE TRUE?

If you are anything like me, you're thinking that God's delight must be reserved for the Billy Grahams and Mother Theresas of the Kingdom. You know, those extraordinary Christians who, by sacrifice and sainthood, deserve an ovation of festive appreciation from God.

The first time I read Zephaniah's words about God's delight, I assumed that the prophet must be talking about the great heroes of the faith—believers like Abraham, Moses, King David, Esther, Deborah—the faithful ones who accomplished enough to make God smile with pride and put a bumper sticker on the back of his celestial chariot that read, "My kids made the honor roll of heaven."

But the truth is, Zephaniah is not writing to the noble but to the nincompoops. Those who deserve the judgment of God have become the recipients of his delight. He doesn't just tolerate forgiven sinners. We who have trusted Christ fill his heart with gladness. He hasn't just made room for us in heaven; he has made room for us in his joyful heart.

DOOM—THE PREDECESSOR OF DELIGHT

The truth is, God's delight wasn't Zephaniah's *only* message or even his *first* message. As the mouthpiece of God, this seventh-century

B.C. prophet was commissioned to pronounce the coming of the Day of the Lord—not as a day of delight, but as a day of destruction. God longed to be generous and gracious, but there was a problem. A few things had happened along the way between Genesis 1 and Zephaniah 3. The chosen people had repeatedly disobeyed and dishonored their God.

The perfections of God were on a collision course with the putrefactions of men. Before there would be any singing, shouting, and dancing for joy in the house of God, a certain question (worth a whole lot more than a million dollars!) had to be dealt with: How can a people who are seeking joy, community, and meaning from sources other than God expect to have fellowship with this holy God—a God who is attended by face-covered angels declaring,

> THE PERFECTIONS OF GOD WERE ON A COLLISION COURSE WITH THE PUTREFACTIONS OF MEN.

"Holy, holy, holy is the LORD Almighty; the whole earth is full of his glory"? (Isaiah 6:1–3).

In Zephaniah's day, God's people were living like morons among morons. Ever since the death of good King Hezekiah, Judah and her capital city, Jerusalem, had been in a spiritual decline. Taking their cue from the surrounding nations, their worship of the one true God had become mere "lip service." Lesser gods had captured their imagination and hearts. God, evermore the righteous Judge of all nations and the jealous Lover of his people, made his intentions quite clear for two and a half of Zephaniah's three chapters. Cosmic judgment is coming!

"I will sweep away everything
  from the face of the earth,"
                declares the LORD.
"I will sweep away both men and animals;
  I will sweep away the birds of the air
  and the fish of the sea.
The wicked will have only heaps of rubble
  when I cut off man from the face of the
    earth,"
                declares the LORD....
"The whole world will be consumed
  by the fire of my jealous anger." (Zephaniah 1:2–3; 3:8)

Ouch! (No wonder I never read the book of Zephaniah completely through until recent years!)

It is against the backdrop of this terrifying woe that an entirely unexpected promise of weal springs forth. Almost shocking our sensibilities, the language of warning and judgment gives way to one of the most exquisite and rapturous descriptions of God's love for his people found anywhere in the Bible. More than sufficient reason is given for us to sing, shout, and rejoice. For God himself is revealed as the one who, out of sheer delight, breaks forth in songs of passionate love and tender rejoicing over a people who are worthy only of his condemnation! The Spirit of Christ in Zephaniah pointed toward a day of unimaginable grace, a day so breathtaking that "even angels long to look into these things" (1 Peter 1:10–12).

THE ORIGINS OF DELIGHT

The book of Zephaniah was not the first to speak of God's delight. His very act of creation proclaims his delight in us. How did I read the first chapter of the Bible for so many years and miss it?

"Let us make man in *our* image, in *our* likeness.... God saw all that he had made and it was very good" (Genesis 1:26, 31, emphasis mine). Moses, the author of Genesis, didn't just give us a trustworthy account of how God created the world. He gave us an inspired revelation of the passionately happy God who didn't need to create anything in the first place!

> IN DECIDING TO CREATE MANKIND, IT IS AS THOUGH GOD SIMPLY CHOSE TO WIDEN THE CIRCLE OF HIS OWN PASSIONATE DELIGHT.

"Let *us* make." God is not talking to angels as he prepares to speak a world into existence, for angels find their origin in God just as do the sun, trees, and people. Neither is he speaking as a ceremonial monarch of Great Britain, "We, the King of England, do decree…" Rather, God is enjoying the unparalleled community of love and joy he has always known as Father, Son, and Holy Spirit. For eternity, he has existed in holy hilarity and glorious contentment as the Three-in-One God. No lack, no limits, no boredom, no contingencies—no "without-ness." *Nothing* can compare with the joy shared within the loving relationships of the members of the Trinity.

In deciding to create mankind, it is as though God simply chose to widen the circle of his own passionate delight and say, "Welcome! Come share in the fellowship of our being and bounty! We have more than enough love and joy to go around!"

Stop and think for a moment. As a child, was your first exposure to God anything remotely close to this image? Mine sure wasn't. Somewhere along the line I got the idea that God created us because he was lonely. How sad! Wouldn't you agree that God could have done a whole lot better in choosing companions?

On the contrary, from Genesis 1 through the last chapter of Revelation, he who freely, lovingly, and joyfully created all things is revealed as needing nothing and giving everything. This makes God's generosity all the more—well, generous—and the call to rich relationship with him all the more astonishing. The origin of our mutual delight is rooted in the rich soil of *relationship.*

Yet how many of us would say that our greatest delight in life comes from a relationship with God? We respect him. We worship him. We read his Word. We try to honor him through obedience. But find our most passionate delight in him? You've got to be kidding! How can such merriment be expected or generated—not to mention, commanded? Yet this was Zephaniah's message—even his decree—for the people of God: "Sing, O Daughter of Zion; shout aloud, O Israel! Be glad and rejoice with all your heart, O Daughter of Jerusalem!" (Zephaniah 3:14).

THE HIGH PRICE OF RELATIONSHIP

But how do we reconcile God's warnings of judgment and his posture of delight? Was God simply "crying wolf"? Did he issue empty threats? Did he change his mind and decide to overlook the many ways his people had ignored and dismissed him? Is he to be compared to a cosmic Santa Claus? We all know that Santa never *actually* brings switches and ashes.

How can God ravenously love a people who are naturally objects

of his wrath (Ephesians 2:3), not objects of his affection? Upon what basis can a thrice-holy God do such a seemingly contradictory thing? No more important question can be asked by any of us.

HE DIED THAT WE MIGHT DANCE.

Jesus is the only explanation for such an amazing love. Zephaniah looked well beyond his sundial and calendar to the day when Jesus the Messiah would come and fulfill a universe-shaping promise made in the Garden of Eden. God, the spurned Creator, revealed himself to be God, the merciful and mighty Redeemer! "And I will put enmity between you and the woman, and between your offspring and hers; he will crush your head, and you will strike his heel" (Genesis 3:15). Out of the sheer magnanimity of his grace, God promised to destroy Satan, who seduced Adam and Eve into eating from the tree of the knowledge of good and evil, and to restore fallen man to himself through a cosmic redemption.

Such a grand restoration required, however, not only the destruction of our archenemy, the devil, but also the fatal wounding of the captain of our salvation, the Messiah—Eve's "offspring." Jesus' death on the cross was the cost of winning an intense battle with Satan. But more specifically, it was the necessary price of our relationship with our Creator. The death of Jesus allows us to look into our Judge's face and see a Bridegroom. This is the heart of the good news, the gospel: Jesus has been punished for our sins so that the floodgate of God's affection can be loosed on us like a healing river! He died that we might dance.

According to Zephaniah, God is free to be generous with his love because he "has *taken away your punishment*, he has turned back your enemy" (Zephaniah 3:15, emphasis mine). A huge barrier has been removed, and a powerful adversary defeated. The wrath of an angry God has been appeased.

THE WRATH OF GOD

But why would God be angry with us in the first place? Is God an insecure, enraged, out-of-control deity like the pagan gods of the nations? No! What, then, is the "wrath of God"? It is the righteous and appropriate anger of the Creator in response to sin—that is, the rebellion, foolishness, and idolatries of his creatures.

> WHILE GOD'S RIGHTEOUSNESS DEMANDED THAT HE BE JUST, IT DID NOT DEMAND THAT HE BE FORGIVING.

God designed us to love him with all of our heart, soul, mind, and strength. Failure to love God as he deserves and demands is the essence of what the Bible calls sin. Sin is falling short of the mark, missing the bull's-eye of his perfect plan for our lives. Certainly, as Creator, God has every right to expect his creation to comply with his design and intent.

For God *not* to judge and punish sin would be a miscarriage of justice and a contradiction of his essential being. In our own court systems, we impeach judges who do not uphold the law and administer justice. But for God to judge and punish Jesus for *our* sins is a demonstration of his immeasurable mercy and grace. While God's

righteousness demanded that he be just, it did not demand that he be forgiving.

THE WRATH OF GOD APPEASED AND ABATED

Biblical scholars and theologians of the cross help us understand the wonder of Jesus' death and the forgiveness it brought as they unpack the concept of *propitiation*. Propitiation comes from a Greek word group *(hilasmos, hilaskomai)* used in four very important texts in the New Testament, all of which reveal the glory and effect of our Savior's death (Romans 3:21–26; Hebrews 2:17; 1 John 2:1–2; 1 John 4:10).

In fact, John even defines God's love by the propitiating death of Jesus. "This is love: not that we loved God, but that he loved us and sent his Son as an *atoning sacrifice* [as the one who would turn aside his wrath] for our sins" (1 John 4:10, emphasis mine). How much does God love us? Enough to put his eternally beloved Son to death in our place! Jesus' death propitiated—that is, appeased and turned away—God's holy wrath.

GOD WILL NEVER BE ANGRY WITH US AGAIN

On the cross, God treated Jesus *as though* he were a sinner so that, in life, he can now treat us *as though* we are righteous.

"God demonstrates his own love for us in this: While we were still sinners, Christ died for us" (Romans 5:8).

"God made him who had no sin to be sin for us, so that in him we might become the righteousness of God" (2 Corinthians 5:21).

What an exchange! God imputed (that is, credited) our sin to Jesus, and he imputed (likewise, credited) Jesus' righteousness to us. Because God poured out his righteous anger on his Son, he will never be angry with us for our sin again. This is almost inconceivable! God will discipline us as a loving Father (Hebrews 12:7–13), but he will *never* punish us as a holy Judge. Justice, mercy, and grace meet at the cross of Jesus. A flood of deserved punishment can now give way to a flood of undeserved affection— toward us, the objects of his affection.

> THE SAME LOVE, DELIGHT, AND PLEASURE THAT GOD THE FATHER HAS FOR GOD THE SON, HE HAS FOR ALL OF THOSE WHO ARE IN CHRIST— NO EXCEPTIONS.

OBJECTS OF HIS AFFECTION

Do you remember the voice that sounded from heaven the day Jesus was baptized by John the Baptist? "This is my Son, whom I love; with him I am well pleased" (Matthew 3:17). God the Father has always loved and delighted in God the Son—and vice versa. Jesus has never been anything other than the Father's pleasure and deepest delight. And it is only because of what he has done for us that we dare speak of ourselves as objects of God's affection and subjects of his great delight. The same love, delight, and pleasure that God the Father has for God the Son, he has for all of those who are in Christ—no exceptions.

Through his perfect obedience to the will of God, Jesus merited God's holy hilarity by fulfilling the law for us—and now God sings

his hilarity over us. And because Jesus suffered the Father's judicial disdain on the cross in our place, we now live in the Father's impassioned delight—forever!

O. Palmer Robertson expresses the incomprehensibility of God's finding great delight and amazing satisfaction in an unlikely people. "That the Almighty God should derive delight from his own creation is significant in itself. But that the Holy One should experience ecstasy over the sinner is incomprehensible.... How could the Holy satisfy himself contentedly in the loving contemplation of the unholy?"[2] Indeed, why does God love his people as much as he says he does? What is the genesis of his love?

In the final analysis, there is only one answer to this question. It was given to Moses centuries before Zephaniah raised his prophetic voice to a wayward world and adulterous people. "The LORD did not set his affection on you and choose you because you were more numerous than other peoples, for you were the fewest of all peoples. But it was because the LORD loved you" (Deuteronomy 7:7–8). *God has made his people the objects of his affection because he has made them the objects of his affection.*

In his sovereign goodness, God has chosen to find great delight in relationship with the ill-deserving. Astounding, isn't it? I never learned *that* in Sunday school! And I never experienced his delight until many years after I'd become a Christian. The journey from the spiritual orphanage to the home of our Father's delight travels through the hamlets and hideouts of our blindness, pride, and unbelief.

*D*ear God,

The pages of this chapter carry words and images that demand a response from my heart. A part of me desperately wants to believe that you are a God of eternal pleasure and happiness and that you do indeed love me with great delight. I get lost in amazement just trying to imagine what that would be like.

But another part of me remains incredulous. Visions of your pursuing love collide with how I have been trained to think of you all of my life. Is it really true? Jesus, did your death on the cross completely pay the price for the many ways I fail you and ignore the Father? Did you actually merit salvation for me by your perfect obedience? I praise you. I thank you.

Make it real to me, God. Help me to really believe that all of my sins—past, present, and future—are forgiven. Help me know for sure that you will never be angry with me again, that your anger toward me and my sin was exhausted on Jesus. Give me power to believe that I am not just one of a ka-jillion sheep that you will take to heaven someday but that I am one of your sons and daughters in whom you find great delight *right now*. I believe. Help me with fifteen tons of unbelief. In the name of your powerful Son, amen.

I PRAY ALSO THAT THE EYES OF YOUR *heart*
MAY BE ENLIGHTENED IN ORDER THAT YOU
MAY KNOW THE HOPE TO WHICH HE HAS CALLED YOU,
THE RICHES OF HIS *glorious inheritance*
IN THE SAINTS, AND HIS INCOMPARABLY
GREAT POWER FOR US WHO BELIEVE.
—EPHESIANS 1:18–19

Be Thou my *Vision*, O Lord of my heart;
Naught be all else to me, *save* that Thou art:
Thou my *best* thought, by day or by night,
Waking or sleeping, Thy presence my *light*.

*E*leanor H. Hull (1860–1935)

CHAPTER THREE

Blind Men Seeing

Whee I was eight, twenty-five cents was enough to get me into the Graham Movie Theater and to buy a big cherry Coke. Of all the rituals of my early childhood, going to the movies stands out as a benchmark of how my imagination defined my realities. And nothing satisfied my thirst like cherry Coke. Ours did not come premixed like the ones filling vending machines or lining grocery-store shelves today. At the Graham Theater, they mixed them fresh on the spot.

Most every Saturday morning, my mom or dad would give me a quarter so I could walk the half-mile to the downtown theater with neighborhood friends. We sat mesmerized and thoroughly entertained by the likes of Hopalong Cassidy, The Three Stooges, Buck Rogers, and a huge assortment of very grade-B monster flicks. And, oh yeah, those were the good old days when you even got a couple of cartoons before the main feature.

THE THRILL OF 3-D

I will never forget, however, the Saturday we saw our first 3-D film. Walking through the turnstile, the ticket tearer gave us each a pair of flimsy cardboard glasses. One lens was red and the other green. I had never heard of such a thing as a three-dimensional movie, so I didn't really know what to expect. After a twin bill of cartoons (pun intended) starring two birds, Woody Woodpecker and the Road Runner, we were instructed to put on our 3-D glasses and brace ourselves for a new experience in movie magic.

Now granted, this was nothing like the technology George Lucas introduced in his Star Wars series, but in the late fifties, it was mighty impressive, especially for those of us in the eight-thousand-citizen metropolis of Graham, North Carolina—a town that still bears a striking similarity to Andy Griffith's Mayberry.

No sooner had the film begun to roll than a strange space creature, resembling a cross between an octopus and a huge lizard, leaped right out at me! Ducking, I yelled with surprise and delight as I unintentionally hurled a box, half-full of Milk Duds, across three or four rows of seats while spilling my cherry Coke all over myself and one of my buddies. Nobody got mad. It was awesome!

For the next ninety minutes, we dodged laser beams, fiery pieces of meteorites, and the slashing claws of extraterrestrial space monsters. Every sensory capacity I had came alive. I even thought I smelled one of those hideous creatures dying, fried by lasers, but then I remembered that's the way our theater popcorn always smelled.

It was the noisiest and most animated movie experience of my life. Everybody was screaming, sliding down in their seats, shifting violently one way or another, yelling warnings to the noble space rangers, and booing the dark villains and monsters from places like Zordok and Sintak. (Maybe pharmaceutical companies watch old space movies to get names for new drugs!)

We weren't at the Graham Movie Theater watching a film; we had been transported into outer space in the faraway year of 2000, when intergalactic travel was commonplace and everybody wore space clothes resembling updated versions of the Tin Man's outfit from *The Wizard of Oz*. How cool. We were there, a part of the story. It's amazing what another dimension will do to your theater experience!

As you would imagine, the good guys prevailed, the space creatures were subdued, and the dark villains escaped into another time warp—that is, until the filmmakers could produce a sequel. After the final credits had run, the projector had been turned off, and the lights had come up in the auditorium, I finally took off my cardboard glasses. I was exhausted and relieved, but also a little sad. It had been so exciting, so real.

Regretfully, everything was predictably and boringly normal again. I wasn't a space ranger, but a lawn ranger who now had to go home and cut the grass with a motorless push mower. How anticlimactic. What an abysmal letdown. I would have stayed through a second showing, but there wasn't one.

The next Saturday morning when my friends and I saw a "regular" movie, well, it didn't quite have the same punch. We had been spoiled. We had tasted dimensions of cinematic magic popular in

the "big cities" but heretofore unknown to previous generations in Graham. Having been taken to a new place, Laurel and Hardy, Gabby Hayes, and the Blob would never again be enough.

Restless discontent and the longings for adventure stirred my eight-year-old soul. Faithfully, I searched the entertainment section of the newspaper every week with great hopes of finding more 3-D movies. Questions of life beyond the boundaries of Graham, North Carolina, invaded my dreams. I wondered, "Is there something better than cherry Coke?"

I Can't Get No Satisfaction

Though not written into any of the New Testament passages on spiritual gifts, there are few manifestations of the Holy Spirit any more important and valuable than the divine gift of dissatisfaction. When God blesses our hearts with boredom, discontent, anxiety, emptiness, or restlessness, he loves us well. For his goal is to wean our wayward hearts away from things that hold no ultimate satisfaction.

Like a decorated French chef offering a free six-course banquet to a Moon Pie–eating generation, God beckons us with incredulous joy to feast at his table of soul delights:

> Come, all you who are thirsty,
>   come to the waters;
> and you who have no money,
>   come, buy and eat!
> Come, buy wine and milk,
>   without money and without cost.
> Why spend money on what is not bread,
>   and your labor on what does not satisfy?

Listen, listen to me, and eat what is good,
    and your soul will delight in the richest of fare.
(Isaiah 55:1–2)

In the theater of his Word, through the care of friends, by the pain of suffering, with the help of all kinds of allies, God pursues and calls to us. "Give ear and come to me; hear

> THERE ARE FEW MANIFESTATIONS OF THE HOLY SPIRIT ANY MORE IMPORTANT AND VALUABLE THAN THE DIVINE GIFT OF DISSATISFACTION.

me, that your soul may live. I will make an everlasting covenant with you, my faithful love promised to David" (Isaiah 55:3).

Amazing. All God wants to do is give us life through his love, at his expense. So how does he do it? How does he get us to grow from Moon Pies to crème brûlée?

COMING ALIVE TO THE MULTIDIMENSIONAL LOVE OF CHRIST

Like most young Christians, I was clueless about the Bible when I first started to read it. But I eventually learned to navigate the landscapes of chapter and verse with relative ease, filling in the lines of my discipleship manuals with duty and diligence. I accepted the importance of regular quiet times and devotional reading of the Word. No real fireworks, but a good foundation was being laid for the future work of the Holy Spirit in me. I would describe my relationship with God in those days as side by side rather than face to face. Important, but not intimate.

Then, as a senior in college, I had my first 3-D encounter with the Scriptures. My status-quo experience of God's love encountered

a rude awakening. By the sheer testimony and power of the Scriptures, I was confronted with a person and a passage inviting a man who was satisfied with watching *The Three Stooges* and eating Milk Duds to a vision of paradise and a feast of perpetual delights. Like the Saturday I saw my first 3-D movie, the apostle Paul staggered my heart with a vision of his journey into the cornucopia of God's love.

> JUST AS WE WILL NEVER EXHAUST ITS SUPPLY, SO WE WILL NEVER COMPREHEND GOD'S LOVE EXHAUSTIVELY.

Right in the middle of one of his most well-reasoned and worshipful pieces of correspondence, the apostle revealed his earnest longings for followers of Jesus in Ephesus—and for his followers wherever you and I live. "And I ask [God] that with both feet planted firmly on love, you'll be able to take in with all Christians the *extravagant dimensions of Christ's love.* Reach out and experience the breadth! Test its length! Plumb the depths! Rise to the heights! Live full lives, full in the fullness of God" (Ephesians 3:17–19 MSG, emphasis mine).

What's with this multidimensional love? Is this just apostolic hyperbole? Has the apostle expounded in doublespeak?

Paul was zealous for all Christians to know the diamondlike prism of Christ's priceless love—a love refracting all the colors of God's generous heart. He spoke of a love *broad* enough to include and reconcile men and women from every people group that has ever existed (Ephesians 2:11–22; Revelation 5:9–10), a love as *long* as eternity and infinity (Ephesians 1:4–5; Jeremiah 31:3), a love *deeper* than the devastating effects of sin (Ephesians 2:1–2; 2

Corinthians 5:21; Colossians 2:15; Hebrews 2:15), and a love *higher* than all we could hope for, ask for, or even imagine (Ephesians 3:20).

Beyond exploring the immensity of God's love, Paul's choice of dimensional language tells us that Christ's love is, quite honestly, incomprehensible, that it "surpasses knowledge" (Ephesians 3:19). Just as we will never exhaust its supply, so we will never comprehend God's love exhaustively—even in heaven! This is important to realize in a day when "the love of God in our culture has been sanitized, democratized and above all sentimentalized."[1]

HOMODIMENSIONAL LOVE

What we have been trained to think of as love in our culture, even in our Christian subcultures, is not so much monodimensional as much as it is homodimensional. We think of God's love almost exclusively in terms of our own privatized experience and self-centered world-view. As members of a consumer-based culture, the overriding concern and preoccupation of our day is "What's in it for me?" "I'll give you fifteen minutes to sell me on the personal benefits of knowing Jesus, beginning...now."

On the contrary, the apostle prayed for Christians, just like us, who already enjoyed a genuine experience of God's love but for whom he desired a greater knowledge of this love. Like a good parent giving encouragement and fueling dreams in the heart of a beloved child, Paul wanted nothing more for his spiritual children than for them to be filled to overflowing with the love of Christ, overflowing to the praise of Christ and the benefit of others.

A GOOD HAUNTING

Paul's consuming prayer (in Ephesians 3) that we know the intricacies of Christ's love has haunted me and invited me ever since I started to meditate on its petitions. I couldn't deny the plain sense of the text—especially as I had to study it at such a painstakingly slow pace with Wright Doyle, my professor of New Testament Greek at the University of North Carolina. Wright generously invited three of us to wrestle through the words of Paul each Saturday in his home. That Bible study rocked my world. Thank God, I still haven't recovered from it.

But as much as I was intrigued with the content of Paul's petition "to take in the extravagant dimensions of Christ's love," I was just as stirred by his story and his passionate soul. His story—as much as his theology—arrested me. Once a Jewish scholar and militant hater of Christians—now a man gentled and emboldened by the mercy and generosity of God—he was alive in a way I knew very little about. In the late sixties and early seventies, I loved to *defend* the faith, but Paul *delighted* in the faith he so courageously proclaimed and defended.

F. F. Bruce, noted New Testament scholar, wrote an outstanding biography of my first real hero and model in the faith titled *Paul: Apostle of the Heart Set Free.* That title said it all! That's exactly what drew me to the *man* Paul—not just to his teaching. His freedom and joy intrigued and convicted me. Here was a man compelled by the love of Christ (2 Corinthians 5:14). I was often compelled by a need to be biblically right, always on time, and never in doubt. But Paul's

48

motivation and power for all things in life, and ultimately in death, was Christ's love for him and his love for Christ.

As I continued to study Paul's life, I began to read the biographies of other men and women who were transformed by the grace of God. Though the details vary, certain themes show up in all of their stories. It has proven to be a source of tremendous encouragement to see how, for most of us, coming alive to God's love is more like a wrestling match than a tea party. Whew! I'm glad I'm not alone.

AUGUSTINE—FROM CONCUBINE TO CHRIST

A father at eighteen, fifteen years with a mistress, nine years of life in a rigorous religious sect called the Manicheans—and his raging passions *still* couldn't be tamed. He had run away to Rome from the faith and home of Monica, his mother, but he couldn't outrun her faithful prayers. Augustine of Hippo (modern Algeria) was finally coming to the end of himself.

Brilliant in philosophical rhetoric but foolish in life, Augustine took a job teaching in Milan, Italy, in 384. It was there that he came under the disruptive influence of God's grace

> AUGUSTINE WAS FACE TO FACE WITH HIS EMPTINESS AND HIS INABILITY TO DO ANYTHING ABOUT IT.

through the ministry of Ambrose, bishop of Milan. First drawn to the gifted bishop because of his reputation as a great mind and orator, the restless Augustine soon became intrigued by Ambrose's heart and the God he served.

For two years Augustine listened as Ambrose preached with

intelligence and passion about the grace of God. Hearing about the beauty and freedom that can be found in Christ alone only highlighted the bondage of Augustine's lustful heart. And the testimonies of others who came to a rich experience of God's love brought even more frustration. Augustine was face to face with his emptiness and his inability to do anything about it.

At last, the thirty-two-year-old Augustine came to the point of crisis and redemptive despair. Walking around in the backyard garden of his home in Milan in August 386, he…better still, listen to his own account of that amazing day:

> I flung myself down beneath a fig tree and gave way to the tears which now streamed from my eyes.… In much misery I kept crying, "How long shall I go on saying 'tomorrow, tomorrow'? Why not now? Why not make an end of my ugly sins at this moment?"… All at once I heard the singsong voice of a child in a nearby house. Whether it was the voice of a boy or a girl I cannot say, but again and again it repeated the refrain "Take it and read, take it and read." At this I looked up, thinking hard whether there was any kind of game in which children used to chant words like these, but I could not remember ever hearing them before. I stemmed my flood of tears and stood up, telling myself that this could only be a divine command to open my book of Scripture and read the first passage on which my eyes should fall.[2]

Wasting no time, Augustine took up a copy of the Bible and read the first passage onto which his eyes fell: "Let us behave decently, as in the daytime, not in orgies and drunkenness, not in sexual immorality and debauchery, not in dissension and jealousy. Rather, clothe yourselves with the Lord Jesus Christ, and do not think about how to gratify the desires of the sinful nature" (Romans 13:13–14).

As though someone had thrown open the curtains and let the bright sunshine into the dark chambers of a castle dungeon, God opened the eyes of Augustine's heart to see the wonders of his love for the sick, imprisoned, and guilty. "I had no wish to read more and no need to do so. For in an instant, as I came to the end of the sentence, it was as though the light of confidence flooded into my heart and all the darkness of doubt was dispelled."[3]

Augustine's words remind me of the scene in which Scrooge wakes up on Christmas morning filled with peace, joy, and freedom. Even better, I think of the words of Jesus, "So if the Son sets you free, you will be free indeed" (John 8:36). By his own testimony, Augustine became a Christian by merely reading two verses of the Bible. He discovered God's amazing generosity in the gift of Jesus. From that moment on, Augustine dedicated all of his intellectual and rhetorical gifts to defending the revelation of God's oversufficient love in Christ for sinners.

OUR NEED IS GREAT, SO WE MUST HAVE A BIG SAVIOR!

Called by many the "doctor of grace," Augustine proved to be a brave and successful warrior in his battles against Pelagius, the British monk who contended that man is capable of meriting salvation by simply following Jesus as an example. Augustine's gospel celebrates a gracious and passionate God doing for man what man could never do for himself.

To be "clothed with Christ" is to accept one's inability to change and find acceptance with God apart from outside help. Augustine faithfully argued from Scripture that the only way we will ever come to freedom is by being realistic about the gravity of

our situation. Our need is great, so we must have a big Savior! Sin, he realized, is a *disease* for which we need a great doctor. Jesus is the physician by whose "wounds we are healed" (Isaiah 53:5). But

"IF I COULD BELIEVE THAT GOD WAS NOT ANGRY WITH ME, I WOULD STAND ON MY HEAD FOR JOY."

Augustine also knew sin to be a *power* over which we have insufficient control. So not only is Jesus our physician, he is also the liberator who has come to break the power of sin and set us free. In addition, he saw sin as a *legal category* that produces *guilt*—because it has to do with God as our Judge. Only in Jesus do we find the pardon and acceptance for which we long.

God gave Augustine eyes to see, a heart to dance, and bread to share with others.

LUTHER—HE LOVES ME; HE LOVES ME NOT

For years, the German monk had lived a tormented life with no assurance or peace regarding God's acceptance and affection for him. "If I could believe that God was not angry with me, I would stand on my head for joy."[4] Even as a young man, every time he found himself thinking about Jesus, he envisioned him as a stern judge, standing over him condemning his sin.

Martin Luther lived under an unbearable burden of fear and guilt as he tried to understand what the Bible meant by "a righteousness from God" (Romans 1:17). How can a righteous God ever enter into a relationship with an unrighteous man? How could *any* man measure up to God's righteous expectations?

If a righteous God promises to accept into heaven anyone who is righteous, is that any different from someone promising a blind man a billion dollars if he can see? Luther's cry became, "How can I find a gracious God?"

In Whittenberg, Germany, in the year 1517, Luther's mourning turned to dancing! Savor his story.

> I greatly longed to understand Paul's Epistle to the Romans, and nothing stood in the way but that one expression, "the righteousness of God," because I took it to mean that right-eousness whereby God is righteous and deals righteously in punishing the unrighteous. My situation was that, although an impeccable monk, I stood before God as a sinner troubled in conscience, and I had no confidence that my merit would assuage him. Therefore I did not love a righteous and angry God but rather hated and murmured against him. Yet I clung to the dear Paul and had a great yearning to know what he meant. Night and day I pondered until I saw the connection between the righteousness of God and the statement that "the righteous one shall live by his faith." Then I grasped that the righteousness of God is that righteousness by which, through grace and sheer mercy, God justifies us by faith. Thereupon I felt myself to be reborn and to have gone through open doors into paradise. The whole of Scriptures took on a new meaning, and whereas before "the righteousness of God" had filled me with hate, now it became to me inexpressibly sweet in greater love. This passage of Paul became to me a gateway to heaven.[5]

Sounds like Augustine and Ebenezer Scrooge all over again! How ironic! The very portion of God's Word that had tormented Luther now brought him a new view of the sufficiency of Christ and meas-ureless peace. The merry monk came to see that the "righteousness from God," which is revealed in the gospel, is a gift of God freely given to sinners.

In Romans 1:17, Paul is not talking about the righteousness that *belongs to God* by nature; rather, he is talking about the righteousness that *comes from God* as a gift. In the gospel, God is not a stern judge demanding us to become righteous by obedience to his law. No, he is a gracious God, providing the very righteousness that his law demands. This righteousness, which he has mercifully provided in Christ, is a "passive righteousness"—that is, a righteousness that comes to us through the gift of faith—not a righteousness that we actively achieve through the merit of our obedience.

Luther used the picture of a mother hen covering her chicks with her wings to illustrate how God clothes us with an "alien righteousness." Where I live, we don't have any chickens, so I'll use a different illustration to explain what caused Luther (and the whole of Western Europe) to dance.

> HE IS A GRACIOUS GOD, PROVIDING THE VERY RIGHTEOUSNESS THAT HIS LAW DEMANDS.

There is a house right up the street from us that is under construction. Actually, it is undergoing a huge remodeling job. A whole second floor is being added on to a ranch-style house. In order to accomplish the project while the family lives downstairs, the construction workers had to cover the entire home with a gigantic tarp. It almost looks like a circus tent.

What Luther finally saw, and what we need to see, is this: To be a Christian is to be accepted by God on the basis of the tarp of his righteousness, which he graciously places over us in Christ, not on the basis of our efforts to reconstruct or remodel our own lives or even the degree to which the project has progressed. In fact, God doesn't only provide the tarp, he is the whole construction team, actively working in our hearts to make us more and more like Jesus. One day the remodeling will be over. Until then, we are already fully accepted by God and acceptable to him only on the basis of the gift of his grace.

I don't know whether Luther ever actually stood on his head for joy, but a fatal blow to the reign of legalism in Western Europe resulted as Luther helped bring the gospel of God's grace back to the church. In so doing, Luther also turned the theological world upside down (make that right-side up) by reaffirming that the Bible alone—apart from all human courts and reasoning—has the right, authority, and power to declare that God has fully and joyfully accepted us in his Son.

WESLEY—FROM STRESS TO JOY

How does one man's honest and agonizing story of coming alive to the compelling love of God impact another, who likewise has little joy and assurance? Three hundred years after Luther, John Wesley—the zealous, hardworking Anglican priest—had more stress than joy as he thought about relationship with God. In the preceding years, Wesley had faithfully risen every morning at 4:00 A.M. to read his Greek New Testament and engage in other spiritual disciplines with "The Holy Club" (sounds scary to me!) at Oxford University in England. He had also engaged in an extensive and exhausting missionary trip to Georgia with his brother Charles—a trip that left him reeling with weariness and painful self-doubt.

As the apostle Paul's story of grace had impacted Luther, so now it was Luther's testimony that intrigued and then captured John Wesley.

A reading from his journal, dated May 24, 1738, tells his story:

> In the evening I went very unwillingly to a society in Aldersgate
> Street, where one was reading Luther's preface to the Epistle to
> the Romans. About a quarter before nine, while he was describ-
> ing the change which God works in the heart through faith in
> Christ, I felt my heart strangely warmed. I felt that I did trust
> in Christ, Christ alone for salvation, and an assurance was
> given me that he had taken away my sins, even mine, and saved
> me from the law of sin and death.[6]

Paul's freedom led to Luther's freedom, which led to Wesley's
freedom—and generations have followed these stubborn and previ-
ously blind men into the IMAX theater of God's Word and grace.

How do we connect with Paul the self-righteous Pharisee,
Augustine the "party animal," Luther the maniac monk, and Wesley
the depressed Anglican priest? Each of these men experienced significant unrest as a prelude to resting in the Father's love. Each became
painfully aware of the irrepressible ache to be set free—the need to
find a "gracious God." All of them honestly confronted the insuffi-
ciency of religion, the bankruptcy of self-salvation, and the almost
unfathomable invitation to experience God's free and boundless
affections in his Son.

What about us? Do their stories indict us or invite us? Hopefully
both.

DISTORTED VIEWS OF GOD'S LOVE

For many of us, our faith is defined by the two Evangelism
Explosion questions: *Have you come to the place in your spiritual journey that you know for sure that if you were to die today you would be*

welcomed into heaven? To that question, many of us can reply with a resounding yes!

The second question is a little more searching: *If you were to die today and stand before a holy God, what reason would you give him for why he should receive you into heaven?* Even to this question, many of us would answer with confidence: "I believe God will welcome me into heaven because, having turned from any attempt to earn his forgiveness, I have placed my trust in his Son, Jesus Christ, who died in my place upon the cross. By his grace I will be welcomed into heaven."

WE SOMETIMES FEEL AS IF WE'RE IN THE HEAVENLY "DOGHOUSE."

If, however, we are asked, *What does God think about you right now, and what can you do about it?* our answers might change with the weather. If we are satisfied with our devotional lives and the amount of time we are reading the Bible, or if we have resisted temptation for a week or two, we would probably respond, "Oh, I think God loves me very much. My walk with him is really strong right now."

When, however, we have been inconsistent in our devotional lives, foolish about what we watch on TV, inconsiderate toward our spouses, or if we are suffering in some way or another, we might say, "God must be pretty displeased with me right now. I know I'm going to heaven when I die, but it wouldn't surprise me if I get a flat tire or something bad happens to me. I need to try harder to please him." We sometimes feel as if we're in the heavenly "doghouse."

Too much of our experience of God's love is tied to our perform-ance, circumstances, and sense of personal well-being. Like a flat cherry Coke, there isn't a lot of fizz in our perception of God's love.

My own personal craving to know God more intimately and to rest more fully in his love has been intensified and complicated by my calling in life. I am a pastor-teacher. I'm *supposed* to have all the answers, assurance, and aura of a man who lives in the unbroken presence of God—or so my overactive conscience is tempted to believe from time to time. For many years, I have lived with the disparity between my theology and my doxology: the words I carefully and authoritatively seek to teach and the truths that should cause me, and all of us, to fall down before God in joyful adoration and willing submission.

It's as though we're reading a 3-D Bible and living a 3-D Christian life without the benefit of the 3-D glasses. All the astonishing truths of God's love are there waiting to come alive, but we aren't wearing the lenses that would enable us to see the riches and depths

THE SCRIPTURES PRESENT THE HEALING OF OUR CARDIO-VISION AS A *PROCESS.*

of his truths. Our vision is "flat"—one-dimensional. The eyes of our hearts need help. We have astigmatism and myopia of the soul! The lively revelation of God's mercies is before us in print, but the truth of it is out of focus, askew, flat, and somewhat blurred.

NEW VISION FOR THE EYES OF OUR HEARTS

More than once I have yearned to have the apostle Paul lay his hands on my head and pray the prayer he offered for the believers in Ephesus:

I keep asking that the God of our Lord Jesus Christ, the glorious Father, may give you the Spirit of wisdom and revelation, so that you may know him better. I pray also that *the eyes of your heart may be enlightened* in order that you may know the hope to which he has called you, the riches of his glorious inheritance in the saints, and his incomparably great power for us who believe. (Ephesians 1:17–19, emphasis mine)

How does God "enlighten" the "eyes of our heart" to see the hope, riches, and power of our great salvation? And how does the Holy Spirit enable us to see more clearly as we long to know the unknowable love of Jesus?

During the writing of this book, I had Lasik surgery performed on my eyes. As a chronic opthomological sufferer, I had nearsightedness in one eye and farsightedness in the other, with a double dose of astigmatism thrown in for good measure. My whole vision was askew. I will never forget the first day after surgery. I walked outside and saw hues, shadows, details, and textures that I had never seen before, even with glasses. Those exquisite details had always been there, but they had been hidden from me. Now I can even see the dimples on a golf ball as I stand over it!

How I wish God had some form of Lasik surgery for the eyes of our hearts—a procedure that would take only a few minutes and that would provide instantaneous healing of spiritual blindness. Wouldn't it be nice just to get zapped on the inside so that we could see everything God wants us to see with perfect clarity and in Technicolor? Though some healings in the Bible were, indeed, instantaneous, the Scriptures present the healing of our cardio-vision as a *process*.

JESUS, SPIT ON *MY* EYES

Throughout the Scriptures, to be spat upon was to be defiled and held up as an object of contempt—as when Jesus was arrested, beaten, and taken to the cross (Mark 15:19). There is one exception, however. In Mark 8 a story is told of a group of caring friends who brought their sightless companion to Jesus, begging the radical rabbi for a healing. Jesus' response is noteworthy:

> He took the blind man by the hand and led him outside the village. When he had spit on the man's eyes and put his hands on him, Jesus asked, "Do you see anything?" He looked up and said, "I see people; they look like trees walking around." Once more Jesus put his hands on the man's eyes. Then his eyes were opened, his sight was restored, and he saw everything clearly. (Mark 8:23–25)

In this story, being spat upon was a sign of affection rather than contempt. Jesus reverses many things! He is free to use anything at any time to accomplish his healing purposes: the majesty of his Word, the singsong of a child, and yes, saliva. Are we above "spit"? Well, how badly do we want to see?

The healing of this blind man corresponds with our spiritual healing and our journey toward greater spiritual sight in at least three ways.

First, we see that the healing we want for ourselves and for one another is not always (in fact, it is never) instantaneous. This blind man experienced a progression in the clarity of his vision. It is predictably the same with us. Now "we see but a poor reflection…then we shall see face to face" (1 Corinthians 13:12). Only when Jesus returns will we "see him as he is," and then we will be made perfect like him (1 John 3:2). For now, we walk in the limitations of faith as we long for the day of sight (2 Corinthians 5:7). Until that day, we will need the ongoing "spit" and touch of Jesus to enable the eyes of our hearts to see more and more clearly.

Second, we shouldn't be surprised when Jesus takes us "outside the village"—that is, outside our comfort zones—to help us see. We have to decide which we prefer: the predictability of our blindness or the adventure of sight.

Last, we can expect God to use our friends as part of our healing journey. I wonder if it was hard or easy for the blind man to have his friends take him to Jesus. I have offered resistance and compliance at different times in my life to those who would help me. But I bet you anything that after he "saw everything clearly," this vision-enhanced fellow found his buddies and worshiped God with them in great delight.

OUR SPIRITUAL EYE CHART

"Which lines can you read? Tell me what you see?" Sitting in the chair of an optometrist, the lights go out and well-chosen images, designed to reveal the true condition of your vision, are projected onto the wall. A new prescription is written based on your ability or inability to discern certain information.

Spiritually speaking, movement toward "seeing" the love of God with 20/20 vision requires greater clarity of the following truths.

First, like Paul and Augustine, we need to see the depth of our need for the mercy and grace of God. Whether we suffer from the unrighteousness of self-righteousness like Paul or the out-and-out carnality and sensuality of Augustine, we tend to be chronically blind to our true condition. How does God move us from simply *wanting* his grace to desperately *needing* it? He uses the standards of his Word (which *only* demands a *perfect* righteousness), the power of his Spirit (the only power sufficient to convict our proud hearts), and the context of relationships (where we generally demonstrate most irrefutably just how selfish and in need of God's grace we really are).

> WE PREFER ALL ATTEMPTS AT SELF-SALVATION TO ABANDONING OURSELVES TO ANOTHER FOR DELIVERANCE.

Second, like Luther and Wesley, we must see that only through Christ can we stand before God in the righteousness he demands. This righteousness comes to us as a gift of grace rather than through any acts of obedience on our part. We are just as blind to the gospel of God's grace as we are to our need for it. We prefer all attempts at self-salvation to abandoning ourselves to another for deliverance. But all such attempts are doomed to failure. We must be able to sing from our hearts, "My hope is built on nothing less (and nothing more and nothing other) than Jesus' blood and righteousness." It is only as we are "robed in his righteousness alone" that we can be "faultless to stand before the throne."

Are you ready for Jesus to spit on your eyes?

To see our need without seeing Jesus is to live in despair. To see Jesus without seeing our need is to live in denial. To see our need *and* see Jesus is to finally live.

How's *your* vision?

*G*racious God,

Reflecting on Paul's freedom, Augustine's peace, Luther's joy, and Wesley's assurance stirs something inside of me. I realize that I am much more passionate about other things than about knowing you. Something is surely wrong when I can get more excited about a larger bank account and a full social calendar than about resting in your love. I have lulled my heart into mediocrity. I am far too easily satisfied. I am a prisoner to spiritual passivity.

Father, please open my eyes to see the depth of my need for your grace. I have no problem in seeing and lamenting the faults and failures of others. Why am I so seldom offended by my own foolishness? Give me a heart that is genuinely sad about the many ways that I do not love you as you deserve. Let my heart hurt when I do not love others as you have commanded. May none of my excuses withstand the convicting work of your Spirit.

Great Physician, you must give me a clearer vision of Jesus. Let me see him as beautiful and as my righteousness—all the righteousness I need in life and will need in death. Cause my heart to believe that clothed in his righteousness, you will never love me more than you do today and that you will never love me less. Continue to rescue me from any attempt to presume relationship with you apart from Jesus.

I am so dull of vision. Open my eyes. Open my heart. Free me to love you as you love me, O faithful and patient God. Through Jesus, who imparts new sight, amen.

DO NOT TURN AWAY AFTER USELESS IDOLS.
THEY CAN DO YOU NO *good,* NOR CAN THEY *rescue* YOU,
BECAUSE THEY ARE USELESS.
—1 SAMUEL 12:21

Jesus priceless *treasure,* Source of purest pleasure,
Truest *friend* to me, Long my heart hath panted
Till it well-nigh fainted, Thirsting after Thee.
Thine I am, O spotless *Lamb,*
I will *suffer* naught to hide Thee,
Ask for naught beside *Thee.*

*J*ohann Franck (1618–1677)

CHAPTER FOUR

The Power of Life and Death

I swaggered up the hall into the main lobby of Graham High School, filled with the excitement of finally being in high school. But I also felt all the tentativeness of being the low man on the totem pole. To be a freshman in high school was a big deal—but not so big to the sophomores, juniors, and seniors. As I got closer to my locker, a first for me in my academic career, I heard a loud voice bark from behind me, "I'd be ashamed if my body was shaped like yours."

At first I pretended not to hear the comment, then I hoped the man behind the voice was talking about someone else. But all doubt was removed when a head football coach walked by, patted me on the rear end, and turned toward me to make eye contact. He just kind of smirked and walked away, whistling up the hall. Welcome to high school, Scotty.

Four years later, when I became a Christian toward the end of my senior year, I read a scripture about there being life and death in the power of words. My mind immediately raced to my freshman year when our coach demonstrated how words can kill.

His comment both devastated and began to define me. Looking in the mirror from that day on, I saw what Coach saw, and it bothered me tremendously. I remembered his words every time I saw my shadow cast in front of me as I walked. Coach's dimensions for the "normal" body composition of a high school young man became mine. From that day on, I knew I wasn't OK. I had given Coach the power of life and death over my view of who I was.

The following summer I decided to "show him." Every day I wrapped plastic wrap around my torso under a sweatshirt and jogged through our neighborhood when the sun was at its peak. Coach lived on our street. I intentionally ran by his house, hoping to be seen. In the three months of that summer, I dropped forty pounds and nearly lost my health to anemia. Coach never cared squat about me, but I had given him power over my soul—power that rightfully belongs only to God.

> I WAS *NUMB, HAPPY,* AND *CONFIDENT*— THE TRINITY I BEGAN TO WORSHIP WITH PASSION AND FAITHFULNESS.

Though I never gained Coach's respect, I did start to get the attention of the opposite sex! With pounds falling off and my hair growing longer (the Beatles had come to America!), I now discovered girls and inherited a whole new set of criteria by which to measure my worth. Holding hands; first kisses; first cigarette; first beer; new clothes to stay current; first car; need for newer, sharper car; prettier girls; longer kisses…does this sound like a slippery slope or what?

But the pinnacle of my life as an "in-the-loop" high school student and the depths of my enslavement to performance-based living began in the summer between my junior and senior year when I joined the band The Originals.

NOT VERY ORIGINAL

"What is this?"

"Trust me, it will give you a lot better buzz than beer. It's grain alcohol mixed with concentrated grape juice."

One cup and I couldn't remember what song we were playing, but I didn't care. I was *numb, happy,* and *confident*—the trinity I began to worship with passion and faithfulness.

I never felt more alive than when I was onstage with my band mates, playing before an adoring crowd that was dancing away to our music. As a seventeen-year-old organ player for a rhythm-and-blues band, I had it all. We played for fraternity parties and clubs up and down the East Coast almost every weekend of my senior year in high school. Adulation, belonging, adventure, applause, a closet full of clothes, a calendar full of dates, a wallet full of money—and yes, alcohol to keep me numb, happy, and confident. So where are you now, Coach?

The problem with living for the approval of people or running from all rejection should be obvious. How do you know when you've done enough or have enough? The "rules" are always changing. There were other bands competing with us for the same jobs. Would we be rebooked or replaced? There were other organ players who had much better "chops" than I had. Was my place in the band secure? Other guys started going after my girlfriends with newer

cars, more money, and better physiques. How could I keep up? It seemed to take increasingly more alcohol to take the edge away from the pain of comparison.

THE "FEAR OF MAN"

Such an unhealthy dependence on people for affirmation traps us in a horrible prison. The Bible calls this dependence "the fear of man." "Fear of man will prove to be a snare, but whoever trusts in the LORD will be kept safe" (Proverbs 29:25). The apostle Paul speaks of the same trap as "trying to win the approval of men" (Galatians 1:10). Jesus called it loving "praise from men more than praise from God" (John 12:43). In more colloquial terms, my spiritual father, Jack Miller, referred to it as "being an approval suck." Being controlled by the "fear of man" is to make people, rather than God, our delight—our great delight.

> WE FEAR PEOPLE WHEN WE GIVE THEM THE POWER OF LIFE AND DEATH OVER OUR HEARTS.

We fear people when we give them the power to make us feel small, insignificant, or shameful. We also fear them when we give them the power to make us feel full, complete, and invincible. We fear people when we give anyone—spouse, boss, children, hooker, coach, abuser, pastor, stranger, *anyone*—the power of life and death over our hearts. Such power rightfully belongs only to God.

TOO EASILY SATISFIED

The truth is, we are far too easily satisfied. In one of his most treasured quotes, C. S. Lewis writes:

Indeed, if we consider the unblushing promises of reward and the staggering nature of the rewards promised in the Gospels, it would seem that our Lord finds our desires not too strong, but too weak. We are half-hearted creatures, fooling about with drink and sex and ambition when infinite joy is offered us, like an ignorant child who wants to go on making mud pies in a slum because he cannot imagine what is meant by the offer of a holiday at the sea. We are far too easily satisfied.[1]

When we give people the ultimate power to be our delight or our destroyers, we are spending our lives making mud pies. As we learn to delight ourselves in the Lord, because of his great delight in us, then we are getting close to what C. S. Lewis meant by "a holiday at the sea."

Think of it this way: The appropriate longings and desires that we have for love and relationship in our world are an echo of our design, not an end. God has made us, first and foremost, for rich relationship with himself. He alone can fulfill the reason for which we have been made. It is *his* joy that we mistakenly hope to find in mere people.

As image bearers of God, the deepest thirst and most acute hunger of our souls is to be delighted in by God. The seventeenth-century Westminster Shorter Catechism states this consuming calling in terms of this question and answer: "What is the chief end of man? The chief end of man is to glorify God and enjoy him forever."

Author and pastor John Piper has appropriately restated this old confession in this way: "The chief end of man is to glorify God by *enjoying* him forever,"[2] and "God is most glorified in us when we are most satisfied in him."[3]

We enjoy God to the degree that we know his delight. When our hearts can say of God with confidence, "I am my beloved's, and his desire is for me" (Song of Songs 7:10 NASB), then are we free to love him with abandonment. And then are we free to love others as God himself loves us.

As creatures of the Fall, however, we tragically put people in the place of God. Instead of learning to love and serve people as an overflow of our rich enjoyment of God and obedience to him, we end up fearing and needing people in very inappropriate and paralyzing ways.

CREATION PRESUPPOSES INTENT

How foolish would it be for your friend to purchase a brand-new lawn mower and proceed to use it to mix concrete? What would you think if your dad used a chain saw to carve a turkey? (All right, no jokes about Thanksgiving last year at your mother-in-law's house!) Or how would it make you feel if your children used your fine china to practice their Frisbee-throwing form? Design and purpose matter. Lawn mowers are designed to cut grass, chain saws are for cutting trees, and fine china is for collecting dust in the china cabinet—I mean, for special meals with dear friends!

> AS IMAGE BEARERS OF GOD, THE DEEPEST THIRST AND MOST ACUTE HUNGER OF OUR SOULS IS TO BE DELIGHTED IN BY GOD.

The Scriptures teach that we are fearfully and wonderfully made. When God created us, he proclaimed us "very good" (Genesis 1:31). Creation presupposes design and intent. God alone has the right to declare our reason for being. The early pages of the book of Genesis reveal that our Lord made us for perfect relationships—with himself, with each other, and with our world. In the Garden of Eden, Adam and Eve knew pleasure, delight, and fulfillment beyond our wildest dreams. Tragically, this quality of life was forfeited through their sin.

Ever since the Fall of our original parents, all of mankind has tried—arrogantly, foolishly, and fruitlessly—to make life work apart from our loving Creator. In far more bizarre and destructive ways than using a chain saw to carve a turkey, we take on roles and goals in life that in time will only fill us with emptiness.

The futility of some of these roles is obvious. The collegian who believes that the chief end of man is to have unprotected sex with as many partners as possible will, in all likelihood, die of loneliness and AIDS. The woman who believes that her role in life is to have a seven-figure salary when she's twenty-five and the figure of a super model when she's sixty-five is setting herself up for huge disappointment—along with a whole lot of stress and plastic surgery. The man who has accepted, as his reason for being, the "calling" of supplying drugs for himself, his friends, and his clients will be jailed, shot, or killed by an overdose.

A LOVE TANK WITH A LEAK

The foolishness and fruitlessness of other counterfeit roles in life are more subtle. In our mainstream culture, one of the most prevailing and popular notions, uncritically accepted, is that each of us is simply a "love tank with a leak." Rather than living as God's image bearers made for rich and rewarding relationship with him and with one another, we see ourselves as primarily needing the love of other people in order to function appropriately or even at all. This is a

concept that many of us have imported into the Christian life. Counselor and professor Ed Welch writes:

> Marriage has been a privilege and blessing to me. It has also been the context for a surprising discovery. I found that being okay in Christ was not quite enough for me. When I was first married, I knew that Jesus loved me, but I also wanted my new wife to be absolutely, forever smitten with me. I *needed* love from her. I could finally handle small amounts of rejection from other people, but I felt paralyzed if I didn't have the love I needed from her, I needed *unconditional* love. If she didn't think I was a great husband, I would be crushed (and, as you might guess, a little angry).
>
> This led to a second awakening. *I suddenly realized that I had mutated into a walking love tank, a person who was empty on the inside and looking for a person to fill me.* My bride was, indeed, gifted in being able to love, but no one could have possibly filled me. I think I was a love tank with a leak.[4]

UMBILICAL-CORD NEEDINESS

What about Bob is one of my favorite movies to watch with my counselor wife. Bill Murray plays Bob, who suffers with "obsessive-compulsive, multiphobic paranoid delusions." He is under the care of an exasperated psychiatrist, played by Richard Dreyfus. In a classic scene early in the movie, Bob tracks down his vacationing therapist and cries out with comedic demand, "I need, I need, I need!"

I have watched the movie at least ten times, and every time that scene appears on the screen, I imagine Bob reaching inside for his umbilical cord and trying as hard as he can to plug it into his therapist. "You must be life for me!" he seems to be crying. (Interestingly enough, Bob ends up being more sane than his doctor!)

Similarly, if we think of ourselves primarily as "leaky love tanks," we will spend most of our lives seeking to be filled up by plugging our own umbilical cords into marriage, affairs, children, fans, friends, etc. *All* of our relationships will become utilitarian. We will tend to look to people almost exclusively as a means of meeting our desire for love and significant relationship. But desire soon becomes need, and need very quickly becomes demand. People begin to take on the power of life and death in our lives. Think of these images as an extension of the "leaky love tank" metaphor:

- People become the oxygen that we need to live.

- People become the electricity to empower our circuits.

- People become the executioners who have the power to take our life.

- People become the cocaine to medicate our pain.

- People become the prophets whose every word is truth.

- People become the priests who have the power to cleanse our consciences and make us feel acceptable.

- People become the kings who control us at will.

Show Me da Money, Power, and Looks

The "fear of man" shows up everywhere in our society. In America, we grow up in multiple contexts and a culture that knows only performance-based acceptability. Virtually everything we participate in teaches and affirms that you get what you earn and that you are what you *do* and *have*. Peer pressure rules—not just among

our teenagers, but at every age level. Our worth tends to be meas-
ured almost exclusively in terms of our performance, acquisitions,
appearance, health, and functional contributions.

Often the first question we ask one another in being introduced
is, "So, what do you do for a living?"—for we define ourselves by
our jobs. When someone dies, it is quite regularly mused, "I wonder
how much she was worth?" Does the thickness of a person's stock
portfolio really establish his or her
value? We often greet one another
with, "Looking good! What have you
been doing to yourself? You make me
feel old and ugly." This casual greeting
carries with it an unspoken but
assumed value system.

> VIRTUALLY
> EVERYTHING WE
> PARTICIPATE IN
> TEACHES AND
> AFFIRMS THAT YOU
> GET WHAT YOU EARN
> AND THAT YOU ARE
> WHAT YOU *DO* AND
> *HAVE.*

In the formative years of my life, I learned well in the school of
performance-based acceptability. I totally bought into the system of
conditional acceptance: from my earliest attempts at Little League
sports to my participation in Cub Scouts—where I competed for
badges and honors with other "cubbies"—to the sometimes praise,
sometimes punishment of taking home a report card every six
weeks. Perhaps I should say that I was seduced into this way of living
and then became a most willing participant and propagator.

DESIGNER GOD

If we see ourselves primarily as a leaky love tank, how will this
affect our view of God and relationship with him? He, too, will take
on an almost exclusively utilitarian role in our lives. He becomes

merely a means to a personal end—the satisfaction of our perceived needs and rights:

- God becomes my masseuse, not my Master.

- God becomes my servant, not my Savior.

- God becomes my lounge chair, not my Lord.

- God becomes my gigolo, not my Husband.

- God becomes my means, not my End.

- God becomes my clay, not my Potter.

- God becomes my scapegoat, not my Glory.

LITTLE GODS WHO LOVED TO BE WORSHIPED

What is it that causes that *whoosh* sound when you open a new can of coffee? It's the sound of a vacuum sucking in air. Anything that has been vacuum-packed is not simply empty; it is aggressively empty. A vacuum seeks, no, *demands* to be filled, and it is not very discriminating about what fills its hungry void. Vacuum rather than emptiness seems to be a more accurate description of the human heart. Thus we cry out with Bob, "I need, I need, I need!" We bring a demanding restlessness into the world from our mother's womb. Legitimate desires and longings are not neutral powers in our souls. Sin has affected everything. By design we are to be worshipers of God, but by nature we have become little gods who love to be worshiped.

The word used most often in the New Testament to describe this condition is *epithumiai* (desires). In Galatians 5:16 the apostle

Paul talks about the "desires of the sinful nature" being at war with the indwelling Holy Spirit. And in Ephesians 2:3 he laments that before coming to faith in Christ, our lives are spent "gratifying the cravings of our sinful nature and following its desires and thoughts."

> ANYTHING THAT HAS BEEN VACUUM-PACKED IS NOT SIMPLY EMPTY; IT IS AGGRESSIVELY EMPTY.

Likewise, the apostle Peter graphically describes how our "sinful desires...war against [our] souls" (1 Peter 2:11). These are just a few of many scriptures that illustrate the groping and demanding nature of the human heart. We are more than empty, but we are also more than vacuums.

IDOLATRY

The most telling and convicting description of the orientation of our unredeemed hearts, found in both Old and New Testaments, is *idolatry*. There is no problem more consistently identified in the Bible than this. The "Greatest Commandment"—like the first two or three commandments from the Decalogue—contrasts fidelity to the Lord with infidelities.

"The open battle with idolatry appears vividly with the golden calf and reappears throughout Judges, Samuel, Kings, the prophets, and Psalms." Thus, the central issue, the most important question to which each of us must respond, is "Has something or someone besides Jesus the Christ taken title to your heart's trust, preoccupation, loyalty, service, fear and delight?"[5]

The fear of man and the delight of God insist that we wrestle with this question—continually.

ASAPH'S JOURNEY TOWARD DELIGHT

How I thank God, once again, for the good gift of his Word! Just when I am tempted to despair of ever changing or getting free from this fear of man, another helpful story emerges in the Scripture to give me—and all of us—hope. What does this journey toward delighting in the God who greatly delights in us look like? He has made us the objects of his affection; how can he become the sole object of ours? Is it easy? Oh, no! Can we make significant progress? Most definitely.

Psalm 73 is the story of a man like any Christian—well, maybe he is a little more aware and honest than most of us. Asaph was a worship leader serving under King David in the Temple. He narrates for us a vulnerable season of his life, a season out of which he could have written the hymn "Come Thou Fount of Every Blessing." Do you remember the line, "Prone to wander, Lord I feel it, prone to leave the God I love"? Asaph shows us what this looks like. The interplay between the fear of man and the delight of God defines his struggle and ours.

"My feet had almost slipped," he began. "I had nearly lost my foothold. For I envied the arrogant when I saw the prosperity of the wicked." Whether out of boredom, carelessness, or watching too many commercials, Asaph started noticing those living the "good life" in his community. Was he chided, ridiculed, or labeled for being a "religious guy"? We have no way of knowing. But peer pressure— the fear of man—did ensnare him.

The "arrogant" and "wicked" ones seemed to "have no struggles" and had bodies that were "healthy and strong." Free from "burdens

common to man" and "human ills," confident, cocky, popular, and without any concern for God whatsoever—they gave every appearance of being "always carefree," and they increased "in wealth" (Psalm 73:2–12).

Do you remember the lyrics of the old rhythm-and-blues song by Dobie Gray, "I'm in with the in crowd. I go where the in crowd goes"? I hear Asaph longing to sing that. Do you relate?

Now for the pity party: "God, what have I gotten from working in the Temple?" he asks. "Surely in vain have I kept my heart pure; in vain have I washed my hands in innocence. All day long I have been plagued; I have been punished every morning" (Psalm 73:13–14). Come on Asaph—"all day long," "every morning"? You've suffered an entire life of empty regret?

Do you see the slippery slope this worship leader was on? Not only did he start to envy (grasp, demand, lust for the "stuff" of those living indifferently to God), but he also slipped into the utilitarian view of God we talked about earlier, asking, "What's in it for me?"

We ask the same question: "I thought Jesus promised an abundant life. Some abundance! Is this all I get for 'seeking first the Kingdom of God'? I'm not sure it's worth all the discipline and effort."

For the moment, Asaph was neither a worship leader nor a lead worshiper. Something other than the love of God was defining him in this instance or season of "temporary insanity." Do you ever go through similar times of envy, doubt, and self-pity? (I ask this question very rhetorically!)

But as for us, so for Asaph: The worship of God called our

brother back to "sanity." "When I tried to understand all this, it was oppressive to me till I entered the sanctuary of God" (Psalm 73:16–17). Let's catch the significance of Asaph's words. He who lived and worked in the Temple did not always enter "the sanctuary of God." It's one thing to go to church but quite another to go to Christ. Aspah once again connected with the One who greatly delights in him.

"What was I thinking, Lord? In my self-centered grief and bitter envy, I acted like a wild beast before you, like a dumb animal, a moron, a nincompoop" (my free paraphrase of Psalm 73:21–22).

> IT'S ONE THING TO GO TO CHURCH BUT QUITE ANOTHER TO GO TO CHRIST.

"Lord this is the truth. I am always with you, because you have me in the grasp of your grace. You are guiding me throughout life's journey by the truth of your Word. I am a foolish man to ignore your revelation. One word, and one word alone, is sufficient to define my future—glory!" (Psalm 73:23–24, paraphrased).

Asaph's next words are as profound a description of a worshiping heart as we will find in the Bible. This is what each of us has been made for. "Whom have I in heaven but you? And earth has nothing I desire besides you. My flesh and my heart may fail, but God is the strength of my heart and my portion forever" (Psalm 73:25–26).

Here is a man who understood and experienced the reality of Zephaniah's words even before they were spoken.

> Sing, O Daughter of Zion;
>   shout aloud, O Israel!

Be glad and rejoice with all your heart,
 O Daughter of Jerusalem!
The LORD has taken away your punishment,
 he has turned back your enemy….

The LORD your God is with you,
 he is mighty to save.
He will take great delight in you,
 he will quiet you with his love,
 he will rejoice over you with singing.
(Zephaniah 3:14–15, 17)

(Have you memorized this passage yet? Go for it!)

Where did Asaph's mini-revival take him? "But as for me, it is good to be near God. I have made the Sovereign LORD my refuge; I will tell of all your deeds" (Psalm 73:28). Fresh delighting in the "rock of ages" led him from envying men (fear of man) to being an emissary of God.

We cannot, we will not, love and serve people as long as we give them the power of life and death over our hearts. As we rest in the love of Jesus, we are freed to love others as he loves us—including our spouses, children, friends, and strangers—and yes, even our enemies. To be delighted in by God enables us to greatly delight in him. We delight in him because he first delighted in us. And as the objects of God's great delight, we are freed to need people less but empowered to love them more. We are conduits, not containers—not love tanks that leak, but vessels of mercy and grace poured out for others.

> AS THE OBJECTS OF GOD'S GREAT DELIGHT, WE ARE FREED TO NEED PEOPLE LESS BUT EMPOWERED TO LOVE THEM MORE.

Tender Father,

I am beginning to understand that you are committed not only to showing me my sins but also to showing me my idolatries. As you do this, my sins seem even more sinful; for I see myself engaged in false worship, not just in making poor choices. Please forgive me and free me from worshiping other things, including people, more than I worship you. And merciful Father, please free me from the worst of all idolatries—thinking of you as other than you have revealed yourself to be.

Jesus, you alone are worthy of all my attention, affection, adoration, and allegiance. I know this to be true, but foolishly, I forget. I am like Asaph. I have my moments, weeks, even months when I want more than who you are and what you provide. Free me from thinking that people can meet the deepest needs of my heart; for in reality, only you can fill me up. Free me from believing that a different spouse (or even having one), different children (or even having some), different parents or friends or church or job or body or anything is what I need the most.

Help me to know you so well and to worship you with such joy and passion that I stop using people and start loving them. You alone can do this, O Lover of my soul. By your grace, through your power, for your glory—forgive my idolatries, heal my wounds, and set this captive free. Amen.

O GOD, YOU ARE MY GOD,

EARNESTLY I *seek* YOU;

MY SOUL THIRSTS FOR YOU,

MY BODY LONGS FOR *you,*

IN A DRY AND WEARY LAND

WHERE THERE IS NO *water.*

—PSALM 63:1

Plenteous grace with *Thee* is found,
Grace to cover all my sin;
Let the healing streams abound;
Make and keep me *pure* within.
Thou of life the fountain art,
Freely let me take of Thee;
Spring Thou up within my heart,
Rise to all *eternity.*

*C*harles Wesley (1707–1788)

CHAPTER FIVE

The Longings of a Thirsty Soul

I t was the look in Bill's eyes that arrested me. His penetrating gaze gave me pause, and quite honestly, rocked me out of my answer-man comfort zone. I've seen the same expression on the face of a friend being rolled away for heart surgery after a final "chat and pat" from his well-trained cardiologist. It's great to have the best surgeon on the medical staff, but as you're being wheeled into uncertainty and a total loss of control, what you really want is the confident face of a friend whose eyes and smile assure you that all will be well. Matters of our spiritual hearts should cause us just as much—no, more—concern as matters of our physical hearts.

As his eyes locked onto mine, his question cut right through to the heart of me: "Are you *sure?*" That's all he said, but I knew what Bill was thinking and feeling because these were the same emotions and questions that had been calling and crying for attention in my

soul for quite some time. But we all have our "mute buttons" by which we temporarily play deaf to the beckoning voice of God.

Through the lens of his soul, I understood Bill loud and clear. I wasn't just looking into the eyes of a brother in Christ; I was being seen by the gaze of my Father in heaven. I saw my own thirsty heart in Bill's.

It was May 1999—almost a year before the initial "unveiling" of my heart—and I had just finished giving my last teaching on Zephaniah's vision of the extraordinary way God loves his children. But Bill wasn't going to let me off easy. He wanted to know if I was engaging in visiting-speaker bombast or if I really believed my own words. Could *both* of us trust what I had been teaching? My first instinct was to respond to his question with platform-speaker confidence and a few well-chosen scriptures, but I couldn't. Though I very much enjoy chatting with people and engaging in "Q and A" after I speak, Bill was asking for a whole lot more than clarification and a hug.

> MY FIRST INSTINCT WAS TO RESPOND TO HIS QUESTION WITH PLATFORM-SPEAKER CONFIDENCE AND A FEW WELL-CHOSEN SCRIPTURES, BUT I COULDN'T.

"Are you *sure?*" That's all he said, but I knew the desire behind the question. *Promise me that I can trust what you are saying, that you're not overstating or exaggerating. Is this* really *what God is like? Does he* really *love like this? If you are hyping me…*

It's a little unsettling to have a microphone in your hand and to realize the responsibility of speaking into people's lives—especially when your talks have been generated more out of your own longings and brokenness than through familiarity and competence. That moment with Bill brought the pain of exposure and the authoritative call of an unexpected subpoena to my fugitive heart.

I was being cross-examined by a loving God: "Scotty, can't you see it? You're like a travel agent accurately describing an oasis you have only seen in a brochure. You point others to the very fountain that you so seldom frequent for yourself. Your words reveal your longings, but your heart betrays your trust. Come, come to me and drink."

THE GIFT OF THIRST

King David spoke for both Bill and me. With pained desire and honesty, the man after God's own heart cried out, "O God, you are my God, earnestly I seek you; my soul thirsts for you, my body longs for you, in a dry and weary land where there is no water. I have seen you in the sanctuary and beheld your power and your glory. Because your love is better than life, my lips will glorify you" (Psalm 63:1–3).

Though I had preached, prayed, and sung the text of Psalm 63 many times, I needed to *experience* what David meant when he proclaimed, "Your love is *better* than life." He wasn't saying "Your love makes life worth living" or "With your love I can do anything"; rather, he was saying "I love being loved by you more than I love being alive." How does one's heart come alive to *this* kind of relationship with God? How can mine? How can yours?

David wrote these words from a hot Judean desert at a time of

great internal conflict and weariness. Among other heartaches, his own son Absalom sought to take David's life. Difficult circumstances and hard providences often become a primary means by which the Holy Spirit quickens our thirst for the fountain that God alone can open up. No one and nothing but God can satisfy the cravings he has placed within the hearts of his children. We are our most sane and free when we live in light of this truth.

> DIFFICULT CIRCUMSTANCES AND HARD PROVIDENCES OFTEN BECOME A PRIMARY MEANS BY WHICH THE HOLY SPIRIT QUICKENS OUR THIRST.

Spurgeon spoke well when he said, "Thirst is an insatiable longing after one of the essentials of life. There is no reasoning with this longing, no forgetting it, no despising it, no overcoming it by stoical indifference. Thirst will be heard. The whole person must yield to its power. So it is with the divine desire that the grace of God creates."[1] It is a gift to be thirsty for God.

Try as we may, all efforts to slake this thirst apart from God are vain, foolish attempts to sabotage our very life supply. But life in a desert holds no guarantees. We are not camels. We can only hold out so long. Eventually, our little canteens will run dry—if we are fortunate, sooner rather than later. It's where we go from there that matters: to "broken cisterns that cannot hold water" or to "the spring of living water" (Jeremiah 2:13).

DISARMING WEAKNESS

What is it about hearing someone's story of struggle and God's grace that is so disarming and inviting? Why is it that our hearts connect much better when we gather in the fellowship of weakness and hope rather than in the arena of competence and performance?

"God moves in a mysterious way, His wonders to perform." Renowned English poet William Cowper (pronounced Kooper) penned these words as a personal testimony, a hymn that tells his story of wrestling with the majesty and mystery of God's work in his painful life and our fallen world. Reflections on God's sovereignty and grace in light of his own personal weakness permeate the treasured works of this sensitive man who became a close personal friend and colleague of converted slave ship captain, John Newton, who penned the words to the classic hymn "Amazing Grace."

The son of a clergyman, Cowper struggled with physical illness and depression most of his life, and at least three times, he attempted suicide. At the age of six, his mother died. And toward the end of his life, Cowper commented that there had never been a day when he hadn't mourned her death. It was to such a heart that God's love became so vital and precious, and it is through such a heart that this same love has been powerfully accessed by other broken men and women.

> WHY IS IT THAT OUR HEARTS CONNECT BETTER IN THE FELLOWSHIP OF WEAKNESS AND HOPE RATHER THAN IN THE ARENA OF COMPETENCE AND PERFORMANCE?

In another of his most popular hymns, "There Is a Fountain" (based on Zechariah 13:1: "On that day a fountain will be opened to the house of David and the inhabitants of Jerusalem, to cleanse them from sin and impurity."), Cowper wrote, "E'er since by faith I saw the stream Thy flowing wounds supply, redeeming love has been my

theme, and shall be till I die." How does the redeeming love of Jesus become the theme not only of a man's poetry, but also of his whole life?

During an eighteen-month stay in an insane asylum, Cowper came upon a portion of God's Word that brought the elusive peace he had always sought. In Romans 3:25–26, he read, "God presented him [Jesus] as a sacrifice of atonement, through faith in his blood. He did this to demonstrate his justice, because in his forbearance he had left the sins committed beforehand unpunished—he did it to demonstrate his justice at the present time, so as to be just and the one who justifies those who have faith in Jesus."

HIS GUILT WAS GONE, BUT NOT HIS WEAKNESS.

This thirsty man found an open fountain in the person and work of Jesus. "And sinners plunged beneath that flood lose all their guilty stains." His guilt was gone forever because Jesus had been punished for his sins, and he now knew himself to be a man declared righteous by God through childlike faith in God's Son. Cowper came alive to God's love at the same age his Savior died—when he was thirty-three years old.

His guilt was gone, but not his weakness. Perhaps this is why Cowper became such a comfort to other sojourners in brokenness. Many of us hear the "nobler, sweeter song" of God's love and his "pow'r to save" when it is sung through a "poor, lisping, stammering tongue" as opposed to any other. I know I do. How about you?

Maybe it's because I am becoming increasingly aware of how much I need the grace of God as I see how little his love actually defines my life. Can we hear it too many times? "God opposes the proud but gives grace to the humble" (James 4:6). That being the case, it shouldn't surprise us when our Father begins to write new chapters of humility in our lives as a means of bringing more grace to bear on the old ones. From where does this fresh grace flow? From one broken vessel to another.

We all naturally despise our weakness, but Paul reminds us that it is through our weakness that God releases his power. Notice the components of his message in 2 Corinthians 4:7:

- "We have this treasure" (of God's love and grace)

- "in jars of clay" (unimpressive, fragile, and ready to be broken)

- "to show that this all-surpassing power" (power to love)

- "is from God and not from us."

WHATEVER GOD MUST DO TO FREE US TO REST IN HIS PASSIONATE LOVE, WE MUST EMBRACE—NO MATTER HOW PAINFUL THE PROCESS MAY BE.

We are not "trophies of grace" to be placed on the mantel for display. We are to become "conduits of grace" placed in the messy world of relationships to serve the forgiving, freeing, healing purposes of God.

So whatever God must do to free us to rest in his passionate love and to share that love with others, we must learn to embrace—no matter how painful the process may be. He is always at work, "his wonders to perform." God is pursuing us in the mysterious and in the mundane, and the wonders he is performing always involve "the wonders of his love."

RESTLESSNESS BUILDING UNDER PRESSURE

Just before my confrontation with Bill, I had finished a season of exhausting activity and intense restlessness—a restlessness that grew almost exponentially as the weeks and months progressed.

Our church had launched a capital campaign in the spring. Now, you need to understand that for *our* church to start a building program was similar to a fifty-year-old man getting married for the first time. Get the picture? We discovered hormones, opinions, and attitudes as a body of believers never before unearthed in our first decade of church life. This season exposed limits and failures in my own life and leadership that were humbling and at times humiliating. There were times when I wanted to run and hide, and to a certain extent, I did. But you can run only so long and so far from the One committed to bringing to completion the good work he has begun in you.

ACCEPTING THAT I WAS POWERLESS TO CHANGE MYSELF BROUGHT A STRANGE MODICUM OF HOPE.

The pace and intensity of change in the church, the weariness of my soul, and the power of the huge secret locked deep in the strongbox of my heart finally began to cripple me. My resources, gimmicks, and coping mechanisms began to fail. Though I had often taught and preached on the apostle Paul's theme of strength in weakness, God was (and is) determined to show me the difference between my theoretical weakness and the real thing.

I was brought face to face with my own misplaced trust and love. Seeing that I trusted in *things* more than *God* hurt. Realizing that I loved things more than I loved Jesus hurt even more. Accepting that I was powerless to change myself brought a strange modicum of hope. Though overwhelmed, I sensed I was being swallowed alive by an enormous providence—not just by a hard set of circumstances—kind of like the fish swallowed Jonah.

SOMETHING SMELLS FISHY

While marine biologists debate what kind of aquatic creature could swallow a man and theologians argue over symbolic versus literal interpretations of the "Jonah tradition," I am gratefully wiping divine fish vomit off of me.

Jonah's story is the tale (real, not tall!) of God's radical commitment to loving at all costs. It shows the extent to which he will go to bring freedom to the hearts of his sons and daughters and his love to the nations of the world.

Long before the fish swims up, God calls Jonah to "go to the great city of Nineveh and preach against it, because its wickedness has come up before me" (Jonah 1:2). Nineveh was the capital city of Assyria, the capital enemy of Israel. Known for their arrogance, opulence, and insolence, the Ninevites were a constant threat to Israel and openly indifferent to the Word and ways of God.

Now you would think that Jonah would relish this divinely appointed chance to heap contempt on those who blasphemed God. The opportunity to pronounce judgment and coming destruction on God-hating pagans had to be, on some level, inviting. But you know the story. Jonah did a "one-eighty" and bought a boat ticket for

Tarshish, exactly opposite the direction of where God was sending him. Why? Maybe he feared for his life? Those Assyrians were notorious for their barbarism.

Nah—that wasn't why he ran away. Later we see the real motivation behind his rebellion and flight to Tarshish: "That is why I was so quick to flee to Tarshish. I knew that you are a gracious and compassionate God, slow to anger and abounding in love, a God who relents from sending calamity" (Jonah 4:2).

Excuse me? You know God to be full of grace, compassion, love, and mercy, so you refuse to obey him, Jonah? What's with that? Does anyone see a slight inconsistency and disconnect here? We get the feeling that Jonah was quoting scriptures about the love of God rather than speaking from personal heart knowledge. (This is getting a little too close to home.)

Jonah became angry because God was thoroughly consistent with the promise he made to Abraham. "As for me, this is my covenant with you: You will be the father of *many* nations" (Genesis 17:4, emphasis mine). God's love is great enough to include Ninevites and their cattle too! (Jonah 4:11). Jonah's love wasn't. His flight and anger revealed a heart in need of, shall we say, a little "tweaking" by God.

FORFEITING GRACE

So, what was the point of all that God did?

- He sent "a great wind on the sea."

- He appointed "a great fish to swallow Jonah."

- He commanded the fish to vomit "Jonah onto dry land."

- He provided a vine to "grow up over Jonah to give shade for his head to ease his discomfort."

- He sent "a worm, which chewed the vine so it withered."

- He provided "a scorching east wind," so that when "the sun blazed on Jonah's head…he grew faint."

Why all these providential disruptions? Why did God orchestrate such a painful pursuit of his son? Why did Jonah need to get swallowed by something much bigger than himself?

Let's allow the man to speak for himself: "Those who cling to *worthless idols forfeit the grace* that could be theirs. But, I with a song of thanksgiving, will sacrifice to you. What I have vowed I will make good. Salvation comes from the LORD" (Jonah 2:8–9, emphasis mine).

> JONAH WAS SWALLOWED BY GRACE, NOT BY A FISH.

Anytime we love something (worthless idols) more than we love God, we forfeit a deeper, richer experience of his grace. And in so doing, we risk bringing upon ourselves all manner of divine disruptions. Why? Because God is mad at us? No! He was "mad" at Jesus on the cross so that we will never have to face the fury of his wrath against our sin.

God will deal with us in disruptive grace because Jonah is right. God *is* "a gracious and compassionate God, slow to anger and abounding in love, a God who relents from sending calamity." Jonah was swallowed by grace, not by a fish.

Who among us, in our right mind, would purposefully rob

ourselves of the enjoyment of God's unconditional favor and love? Such is the insanity of sin and the foolishness of our hearts. We will either cling to our worthless idols, or we will cling to the Lover of our souls. We either satisfy our souls' thirst with living water from the fountain of God, or we run after temporary pleasures that leave us thirstier still. So great is God's love for us that he will not allow polygamy to reign in our hearts for very long. And we are naive to assume that we can love God and refuse to love what he loves.

Abraham Kuyper, former prime minister of the Netherlands, once commented that God can pay us no greater compliment than being jealous for *our* love. As the husband of his beloved people, God disciplines us as a way of regaining our hearts—not as a means of casting us away. What a revolutionary perspective: God disciplines us to remove the obstacles to our enjoyment of his love for us and to free us to love him more fully and faithfully.

Indeed, he will arrange circumstances of his own choosing to bring us to our senses and to his embrace.

CLINGING TO NONSENSE

What was it that moved God to rearrange the waters, weather, and the animal and plant worlds to assist him in speaking to his reluctant prophet and son? What were the "worthless idols" to which Jonah clung so tenaciously? Here's a few that occur to me as I look at Jonah's life:

- nationalism

- racism

- vengeance

- unforgiveness toward the Ninevites

Just how tightly did Jonah cling to these idols? Like Super glue! The thought of the Ninevites coming to know the mercy of God made him so angry he wanted to die! "Now, O LORD, take away my life, for it is better for me to die than to live" (Jonah 4:3). What made life seem so worthless to Jonah? He couldn't stand the thought of seeing the Ninevites loved by God!

Amid Jonah's pantheon of idols were *autonomy* and *arrogance toward God*. Can these be idols? *Anything* can be an idol! Jonah's heart was so at odds with the ways of God that he again pled with God to let him die when a vine that God himself had planted for Jonah's comfort withered! (Jonah 4:9).

When we make ourselves the object of our affection and when we pray, "My will be done," *anything* that stands in our way angers us, and the true condition of our hearts is exposed. (Isn't it fun to identify other believers' idols?)

HEART-WAY ROBBERY!

Along with idolatry there are other things that cripple our hearts and stifle the gladness and joy that the God of Zephaniah intends us to have. What else robs our hearts? Why do we struggle or simply move on to other and lesser vocations than knowing the love of God? Looking back over my past and into the present as a contemporary Jonah, I can see several thieves that keep us doubting, dodging, and denying God's affection.

We have nothing in the whole of life with which to compare the love of God. God's love is unique. It simply seems too good to be true. But God's love is the foundation of all other loves. Unfortunately, we tend to define the archetype by the types; we confuse the shadows with the substance. For instance, we take our experience of our earthly father's love and project it back onto God, when in reality we need to look first at God our Father to see what an earthly father is meant to be.

Painful events in life make it difficult for many of us to believe that God is love. The stories of betrayal, abuse, abandonment, chronic pain, and unimaginable suffering cause many to doubt God's love. We blame God for the evil we see in the world rather than blaming the evil one who reigns as ruler over this temporal earth (John 12:31; 14:30; 16:11). We have a hard time waiting for the day when God will redeem every fear, heal all sorrow, and make everything new (Revelation 21:1–5).

We have minimized our sin to the point that God's love is either assumed or deemed irrelevant. Ours is a culture of victims who make excuses rather than agents who accept responsibility for the many ways we fail in love. It is only as we come to discover how ill-deserving we are of God's love that we can be stunned and grateful for such radical acceptance and tenderness from him.

Many are paralyzed by shame and self-contempt. On the other end of the spectrum, there are many who are seemingly unable to believe that God is merciful and gracious. The condemning work of Satan and a fragile conscience anchor their hearts to self-absorbing despair.

We are legalists to the core—living lives defined by performance-based acceptability. Only the Holy Spirit can free us to know that

God's lavish love cannot be earned by any of us. It is a free gift given to us on the basis of the finished work of Jesus Christ. As Jonah learned (and quickly forgot!), "Salvation is of the Lord."

We are far too easily satisfied by other loves. Like Esau, the demand for instant gratification seduces us into settling for a bowl of stew in the place of our Father's inheritance. Such is the curse of consumerism and the demanding nature of our fallen hearts.

We demand the right to define love. Like a self-centered teenager saying to his vulnerable date, "If you really loved me, you would sleep with me," so we arrogantly try to manipulate God on our terms. "If you were really a God of love, you would_____."

THE DEMAND FOR INSTANT GRATIFICATION SEDUCES US INTO SETTLING FOR A BOWL OF STEW.

We suffer from wrong or incomplete teaching. Blasphemy is to misrepresent God in any way, to distort his name and image. The truth of God's Word sets us free. The distortions of wrong teaching enslave. Incomplete or false presentations of the gospel do not merely maim our hearts, they destroy them.

Many of us foolishly refuse the feast of the Father's affection. God has given us the means of growing in his love. He invites us to the banquet of his tenderness, freely spread for us in the Scriptures, worship, fellowship, prayer, and service. To ignore his table is to suffer the consequences of an malnourished soul. Not only do some of us not know where to find the book of Zephaniah in the Bible, we didn't even know there was such a book or such a love!

Undealt with wounds from the past can limit and distort our experience of God's love. Like a broken bone that was never set, a broken

heart, in time, can throw everything out of whack and define how we walk or limp through life and the knowledge of God. It is as we learn the relationship between our sinfulness and our woundedness that we begin to understand how our hearts serve, as John Calvin said, as "idol factories." We create substitutes for the love of God and the God of love. I know this pattern all too well.

Before you go on to the next chapter, go back through this list and note which ones possibly represent obstacles in your journey. What is keeping your heart from the feast of richest fare?

Not-So-Idle Idols

Jonah's story encourages all of us to take the necessary time to reflect on *our* stories. Having been recently "swallowed" by a fish of God's choosing, I have been asking our heavenly Father to show me *my* worthless idols and crippling attitudes and behaviors. Ouch! He is gladly complying!

But as painful as it has been to see the misplaced trust of my heart and the not-so-idle idols that reside there, on the route to brokenness I strongly sensed that the Lord was with me. He showed himself to be mighty to deliver my foolish heart—and he is still doing so, for "salvation comes from the Lord." As I began to taste a measure of his delight, his love started to bring stillness to my restless heart.

Before you go to the next chapter, think back over *your* story. Identify times in your life when God has gifted you with a thirsty soul. Then take the next step and uncover your idolatrous attempts to satisfy that thirst on your own. Are you ready to tear down the idols in your heart and relinquish your all to the mighty God of grace? Are you determined to stand up to Satan's attempts to rob you of God's joy? Your journey will include some uphill travel as you experience the "severity of his mercy," but the reality of relationship with your creator will fill you with unimaginable joy.

Dearest Father,

Thank you, powerful God of providence. You arrange the circumstances of my life to drive me to you. I fight, I whine, I try to rebuke as demons what you actually send as messengers of grace. I have heard that you whisper in blessing and that you shout in adversity. This is true in your Word; let me accept it as true in my life. So great is your love for me that, as with Jonah, you appoint various fish to swallow me and bring me to the shore of mercy and understanding. Give me a willing heart.

Help me discern your smile behind the hard providences in this current season of my life. Help me see what you are trying to teach me through the very things I am attempting to run from. To what worthless idols am I clinging? How is my pride keeping me from the grace that could be mine? Even as I offer these petitions, I am aware that I love my comfort more than I trust and adore you. Forgive me.

And forbearing Father, please show me other thieves that have robbed my heart of your grace. No doubt, I have aided and abetted some of these robbers. For that I ask your forgiveness. Other enemies of your affections have pillaged my heart; please help me recover that I might live as a child of mercy wherever you send me. In the name of your Son, I petition you. Amen.

FEAR NOT, FOR I HAVE *redeemed* YOU;
I HAVE SUMMONED YOU BY NAME;
YOU ARE MINE.
WHEN YOU PASS THROUGH THE *waters*,
I WILL BE WITH *you*.
—ISAIAH 43:1–2

Every *joy* or trial falleth from above,
Traced upon our dial by the *Sun of Love*;
We may trust Him fully all for us to do;
They who *trust* Him wholly
Find Him wholly *true*.

*F*rances R. Havergal (1836–1879)

CHAPTER SIX

The Severity of God's Mercy

D o you want to get well?"

A crowd of disabled people was gathered at a pool in Jerusalem called Bethesda (John 5:1–15). According to a certain tradition, an angel of the Lord would come down from heaven and stir up the water. The first person to get into the water was healed. Our Lord singled out a man who had been an invalid for thirty-eight years and asked, given the circumstances, what seemed to be a rather odd question: "Do you want to get well?"

Why wouldn't he want to get well? Why would he gather with others at this very spot if being freed from his infirmity wasn't the goal? The truth is, healing has its consequences. A Middle Eastern beggar made a pretty good living from alms. If healed, this invalid would have to learn a whole new way of living. Cure can be scary.

Similarly, as I began to deal with my own thirty-nine years of heart paralysis, the thought of freedom thrilled me, but it also intimidated and threatened me.

After my unexpected confession to my friends Scott and Mike that I hadn't been to my mother's grave in the thirty-nine years since her death, I was finally ready to go.

Her grave site was about eight hours from our Nashville home. As Darlene and I planned our trip, we decided to stop at a friend's vacation home in Sugar Mountain, North Carolina, for a few nights, then drive on to Burlington, where my dad and stepmother live. It so happened that my brother, Moose, and his wife, Sue, had planned a trip to Virginia the same time we were going to North Carolina. Loving me well and wise to the ways of my foolish heart, Darlene got an idea.

"Honey, what do you think about Moose and Sue spending a night with us at Sugar Mountain to break up their drive to Virginia Beach? I'll ask Sue to bring the pictures of your mom and some of your parents' love letters. It might be great preparation before going to your mom's grave." Somewhat reluctantly, I agreed. You can't imagine the depth of my self-protection and control. Not only had I avoided Mom's grave, I even refused to offer more than a glance at her portrait that hung in Moose's dining room.

The idea of sitting still and slowly looking at pictures of my mom, while now inviting to me, also brought great threat. And the thought of reading those letters… What would that feel like? What memories would it stir up? What would be required of me? Where, in time, would this lead?

But the plans were already in motion. Moose and Sue would be here any minute.

"We're here!"

After putting their overnight things in the downstairs bedroom, Moose and Sue joined us in the family room. I assumed that the little leather carrying case he brought up and put on the card table contained the "goods." We visited for a while, and then they went on to bed, tired from the day's long drive.

I opened the latches one at a time while Darlene straightened up the kitchen. Why did this feel as if I were opening Pandora's box? Lifting the lid slowly and deliberately, I pulled out a large envelope, which contained a thick stack of old photos. Beneath were about thirty letters held together by a couple of now-brittle rubber bands.

As I slid the pictures out from the old manila envelope, my heart began to race and then…there she was. I saw my mom's beautiful face for the first time in so many years. I really saw her. My tears flowed, and I felt no shame at all. There she was, sitting on a pile of rocks along the coast of North Carolina, facing a sea breeze I could almost feel. With her shoulder-length brunette hair pulled back in a ponytail, she looked every bit a calendar girl. "Honey," I called to Darlene, "come and see my beautiful mom." I was so proud to introduce my wife of twenty-eight years to the woman she never met, even as I was being reintroduced to her myself.

THE SMILE

I could not take my eyes off my mom's smile. I still can't. In fact, that's what stands out in all the pictures of her. Her whole being

beamed with life and a light that made everything OK. Feelings of loss and joy overwhelmed me, even as they do now. *This is the woman I've missed for thirty-nine years. This is the awesome lady whose laughter was infectious, whom everybody loved. My mom.*

I couldn't stop. My mind started running to events of my life we hadn't shared but should have. What difference would it have made to have her walk with me during those crazy adolescent years when everything was changing? It would have changed everything! I felt so alone and clueless much of the time, as I tried to figure out the mysteries of life. I missed so much. I missed her.

Oh, to have had this cool lady bug me and dote over me about girls and pick out flowers for my junior prom date. For her to have been there when I finally gave my heart to Jesus, to celebrate my high school graduation, and to get me ready for college. To send letters and care packages while I was in Chapel Hill, reminding me to go to class and telling me how proud she was of me.

Then when Darlene came along, what would it have been like to have Mom give me wisdom about love, romance, and the heart of a woman? Would I have listened? How would it have felt to have her make out the invitation list to our wedding and straighten my bow tie on my wedding day and kiss me on the cheek, to dance with her at the reception? Friendship between Darlene and Mom—it would have been so amazing for both of them. I thumbed through more pictures...more smiles...more thoughts...more tears. What a grandmother she would have been. My kids would have adored her and she them.

I wasn't prepared for the juxtaposition of grief and freedom that welled up inside of me, a strange tandem indeed. As I sat there on the couch with Darlene and my mom and the sounds of a mountain stream filling the room, it hurt so bad but felt so good. I couldn't help but feel a certain amount of remorse and deep regret. I asked then and I am still asking, Why did it take me so long to do the very thing necessary to confront the restlessness of my soul? Why had I waited so long to start the process of grieving—not so much her death, but the loss of her life?

> WHY DID IT TAKE ME SO LONG TO DO THE VERY THING NECESSARY TO CONFRONT THE RESTLESSNESS OF MY SOUL?

What a prisoner I had been—so enslaved, so paralyzed, so fearful, so alone. So this is what Dan meant seventeen years ago when he told me that the love of God didn't define me nearly as much as my mom's death and my busy, noisy heart.

ANGER

Quite unexpectedly, I started to get mad. Feelings of anger began to well up inside of me, feelings I had fought and denied for thirty-nine years. Historically, I do sad a whole lot better than I do mad. Sad is a lot safer, or so I reasoned. *Anger is destructive; it hurts people,* I told myself over and over—especially after I became a Christian. That belief became a law and a lie of my heart.

I feared anger in me and toward me, and ever since Mom's death, I've tried my best to control any expression of this potent

emotion in my world. When Philip Yancey's book *Disappointment with God* was published, I remember, quite paradoxically—no, make that hypocritically—getting angry. (Though I didn't *call* it anger; I called it righteous indignation.) For some strange reason, I felt the need to defend God's reputation, as though he needed it. I also feared the possibility of falling into a victim's mentality, blaming all my foolish choices on the death of my mom.

Who does Yancey think he is writing a book that encourages Christians to shake their fists at God and vent? Doesn't he know anything about the sovereignty of God? Isn't Jesus enough? All we need is a bunch of whining believers running around complaining about how badly God has treated them. Obviously, I hadn't read the book.

Suddenly I flashed back to the many times I had tried to reason Darlene out of the growing sense of anger she felt when her dad died. Quoting Scripture, having her prayed for, giving her books and tapes on anger and depression; I grew weary of how long it took her to "get over" Phil's death. At the memory, I started to feel sick.

Maybe it wasn't Darlene's anger that I feared as much as my own. What was I afraid of? Going out of control? Becoming a raging maniac? Becoming an atheist?

> WHAT HAD I EXPECTED GOD TO DO IF I EXPRESSED MY ANGER?

By now I couldn't deny my own feelings of disappointment and anger. I didn't want to stuff them any longer. *This is the great lady I have missed. Look at her. It's not fair; it's just not fair. I hate it! God, why?* It wasn't her death that I needed to grieve the most; it was the absence of her life. I am a different and a difficult man to a large extent because of having my mother ripped so harshly out of my life at age eleven. I needed to see this—say it—and sit in it for a while.

For all those years, what had I expected God to do if I expressed my anger? Had I thought he would be shocked, that he would glare at me with a disapproving scowl, that he would withdraw from me? Now I understand that God wouldn't have been affronted by my anger; he wouldn't have struck me down for my honesty. We feel what we feel. I should have known him better than that—but I did not know him as well as I thought.

WHATEVER YOUR FURY, IT IS ONLY A SPECK OF WHAT GOD FELT AND DELIVERED AGAINST HIS SON FOR YOUR SAKE.

After all, it wasn't Job, but the friends of Job, who were charged with misspeaking about God. I now see something terribly beautiful and godly in those long, hard seasons of anger Darlene went through in response to her dad's suicide. Her tears and passion were similar to those shed by Jesus outside of the tomb of Lazarus.

The Greek text of the phrase, "Jesus wept" (John 11:35), speaks of great agony of soul, not just the sadness of confronting a personal loss. He who created Lazarus and who in a few moments would raise him from the dead demonstrated his pure hatred of sin, death, and evil. God's original design for creation did not include the death of a friend, mother, or the suicide of a father. To hate the effects of the Fall—any manifestation of how sin and death have perverted God's original design—is surely an act of worship. And surely, such anger is meant to intensify our longing for the day when all sin, death, evil, sickness, and tragedy are gone forever.

Such appropriate anger is meant to teach us about the cross.

Whatever your fury, it is only a speck of what God felt and delivered against His Son for your sake. If your rage compels you to smash your fist on a table, consider the blow as a reminder of what the Father already carried out against the Son. What kind of God is He, to turn His fist-smashing wrath against Himself rather than against you? Awe of God must grow if our anger is to deepen in the direction of righteousness.... Our anger is always pitifully small when it is focused against a person or object; it is meant to be turned against all evil and all sin—beginning first with our own failure of love. In order to deepen righteous anger we must learn what it is to join the anger of God.[1]

GROUNDHOG DAY

The next morning, Darlene and I started out for Dad's house. As we drove I kept thinking about the family photographs. Although most of the pictures Moose brought were simply of our mom, he did include one of our whole family. Mom stood on the far left, smiling of course, while Moose and I sat balancing on top of a white picket fence with Dad on the right. One detail of this picture arrested my attention. My dad's right hand was resting on my left, three-year-old foot, apparently making sure I didn't fall off the fence while the photo was being taken. It felt so strange to see his touch captured on Kodak paper, for I don't have a single memory of my dad *ever* touching me, in discipline or in affection. Why the absence of such remembrances? Surely, there must have been many times we touched...right? But so complete was our disconnection after Mom's death, I guess I assumed it had always been that way.

In a moment of bravery and imagined confidence, I had actually considered telling Pop about the pictures and seeing if he wanted to come with me to Mom's grave. But as we got closer to his house, I went from six-foot-one to about four-foot-two and from fifty years old to about fifteen. Not yet. To confront one's family system requires much grace, more than I had at the moment.

As we drove into my dad's driveway, I thought of the Bill Murray movie *Groundhog Day*. In this film Bill Murray's character is caught in an endless cycle of repeating the same twenty-four hour period over and over and over. The alarm clock rings, and the events of the day unfold just as they did the day before. Everything is predictable. Everything. The perpetual nightmare ends only when Bill Murray finally figures out how his own choices can alter the dysfunction of his life and the quality of relationship he enjoys with his romantic counterpart, played by Andie MacDowell.

For years I have lived the heart of that story line with my dad. Everything about our visits is so predictable: where we sit, what we talk about, how long we visit, when we eat. So regular, so safe, so controlled, so empty. I never saw it as a nightmare, however, but as "better than abuse," "better than many people, if not most, have in life." How many times have I rehearsed this tired and worn monologue? Who was I trying to convince with this superficial soliloquy? Like the child who comes home from school with a C on his report card who only thinks of comparing his mark to his peers who made Ds and Fs, I chose my comparisons well.

"Well, well, look who's here." My dad always gave that same greeting when we came in the back door—*always*. Raw from the

previous night's emotion, I simply couldn't play out the same old same old. Intentionally I sat in a chair I'd never sat in and took our conversation in a direction outside our predictable triad of topics—sports, weather, and the economy. It wasn't revolutionary, but it was a start. As we shared lunch, my mind raced toward the main event of the day—going to Mom's grave.

A GRAVE DAY

Standing over her grave, supported by Darlene, I tried to pray. "Mom, I mean, Lord…" I wanted so badly to talk to her one more time. We never got to say good-bye. That hurt so bad. As I wept, I tried again to pray. "Lord, I miss her so much. Thanks for…" That's about all I could get out. More tears, sadness, and buried longings coming alive. But this was just the beginning of one of the most emotionally charged afternoons of my life.

Only two or three hundred yards south from where we stood, on the other side of a large praying-hands monument, Darlene's dad is buried. We made the short walk. Phil died in July 1976, only a month after the birth of our first child, Kristin. Tragically he had taken his own life after a long fight with alcoholism and a short season of coming to faith in Christ. Darlene wept quietly as I fought feelings of guilt. I remembered how poorly I had loved her during one of the greatest crises of her life. My refusal to deal with Mom's and Debbie's deaths made it almost impossible for me to deal with Phil's or to enter into Darlene's pain. I had been, for the most part, emotionally absent during the gut-wrenching, faith-shattering grief she went through as she tried to make sense of God's good gift of our first child and the nonsense of her dad's suicide. The prison of my self-protection looked uglier and uglier.

Only God could have orchestrated such a moment and in, of all places, a cemetery—for everybody a place of death—for Christians a place of death and hope. Within a span of two hundred yards and ten minutes, I was confronted with my most painful and defining moment in life, my greatest failure in love, and the promises of the God of resurrection.

> SOMETIMES IT'S EASIER NOT TO HOPE, ESPECIALLY IF YOU ARE TERRIFIED OF THE POSSIBILITY OF MORE PAIN.

Dare I hope? Sometimes it's easier not to hope, especially if you are terrified of the possibility of more pain.

Tenderly holding hands, we walked to our car and quietly drove twenty minutes to yet one more cemetery. Pulling into the well-kept Quaker burial grounds, I didn't have to stop and get a map from the office. We had been here very recently, and the grave still wore its telling signs of newness. Only three months earlier, November 1999, I had preached the funeral service for Darlene's mom. We committed Mary into the hands of the Savior she loved so much after a bout with heart disease.

Standing at Mary's grave, I actually felt a little hope in an otherwise very sad afternoon. The Holy Spirit had been at work in my own diseased heart in the last season of Mary's life. God brought a good measure of reconciliation and healing between mother-in-law and son-in-law. Our relationship had not always been easy. But in the last few years—and especially in the last three months of her life—things softened and changed between us.

Holding Darlene close, the sights, sounds, and smells of Mary's final hours all came back to me with intense reality. In the midst of medical chaos, we spent her last afternoon in this world together holding hands, reading the promises of God, and worshiping Jesus. I remembered our feeble but sincere attempt at singing the doxology as Mary breathed her last breath.

REBREAK

We aren't masochists. Really we aren't. Neither Darlene nor I had planned for this afternoon to be so gut-wrenching. Who in their right mind would? But this is exactly the day I needed. God loved me so well that painful afternoon. He showered me with "severe mercy." His pursuing heart was never more evident. The promise of the quieting effects of God's love only makes sense to those who have disquiet in their minds and hearts. I more than qualify!

> JESUS IS NOT ONLY THE WOUNDED HEALER; HE IS ALSO THE WOUNDING HEALER.

My friend Paul is an orthopedic surgeon. I once asked him what happens to a person who breaks a leg and never gets medical attention and the broken bone never gets properly set.

"Well, the body has a remarkable ability to heal itself, Scotty. But in time, this man's whole muscular-skeletal system will get out of whack, and he will be miserable. He'll end up in my office, and I'll probably have to rebreak his leg and then set it so proper healing can begin."

I didn't have the stomach to ask Paul how that little piece of surgery is accomplished. Visions of a large hammer and chisel came to mind.

As painful as the idea of rebreaking a leg sounds, if that is what it takes to heal a miserable man, it's not too great a price. Haven't we all heard of a loving shepherd who sometimes has to break the leg of an errant lamb or goat in order to retrieve this member of the flock and bring it back into the fold? God works in our lives in a very similar fashion. If the breaks in our hearts don't get the attention they need, we will manage to heal a little, but it won't take long for our whole relational systems to get out of whack. And God will set about rebreaking our hearts. He wounds that he might heal. It hurts so badly, but it leads to freedom.

God's grace is for the needy and his mercy for the miserable. Jesus is not only the wounded healer; he is also the wounding healer. As we go deeper into God's love, you and I will learn to say thanks for such severe mercy and painful grace.

GOD'S SEVERE MERCY

We come again to Zephaniah's words of promise, love, and hope, for they were spoken to a people who needed to be broken. The people of God in Judah, and in Jerusalem in particular, had grown oblivious to their true condition. Their hearts had grown cold toward the Lord, indifferent to his covenant demands, and—in short—they had become like all the nations around them. It is under such circumstances that God's severe mercy begins its work in

his sons and daughters—and he does so *because* he loves us, not because he has stopped loving us.

God is determined to change our hearts, not just our habits. He is tenaciously committed to having a people who, one day, will be made perfect in love—a people who will love perfectly forever. But how can we sustain the demands and intensity of the metamorphosis of his severe mercy? We become restless and weary in the journey of change; we have little peace and less hope that we will ever be different. In unbelief, we wonder if we will ever be free.

But to a disobedient and undeserving people—just like us— Zephaniah declares of our God, "The LORD your God is with you, he is mighty to save. He will take great delight in you, *he will quiet you with his love,* he will rejoice over you with singing" (3:17, emphasis mine).

> TO SEE OUR SINS, WOUNDS, IDOLS, AND FAILURES APART FROM GOD'S GRACE IS SIMPLY TOO MUCH.

Though the Hebrew of this phrase can be translated in different ways, Martin Luther seems to have captured the intent of the text. "He will cause you to be silent so that you may have in the secret places of your heart a very quiet peace and a peaceful silence."

This is the peace that passes all understanding—a peace that is often only gained after passing through the severity of his mercy. This is the stillness the psalmist proclaimed when he cried, "Be still and know that I am God" (Psalm 46:10). God does not bark at us in frustration, "Shut up and sit down! When are you going to get your act together? Why is it taking you so long?" No, he quiets our hearts in and with his powerful and limitless love.

Larry Lee Walker offers another helpful interpretation of Zephaniah's words: "The Lord's love will be so strong and deep as to hush motion or speech; there will be silent ecstasy." There is only one power and presence sufficient to change us and sustain us in the process of such a radical—and often painful—transformation: the quieting love of God.

To see our sins, wounds, idols, and failures apart from God's grace is simply too much. We will either minimize our condition, thus marginalizing our need of grace, or we will run away in hopeless despair to the arms of a lesser love or to the worship of lesser gods.

But God pursues us in our restlessness, receives us in our sinfulness, holds us in our brokenness, and frees us from our lovelessness. It is both irony and providence that my experience of these great truths intensified and solidified *after* committing to write this book.

As hard as I had worked for the past twenty-two years as a Christian to put a "godly spin" (what an ugly phrase) on Mom's death, the spin had been bigger than God in my life. That's what the Bible calls idolatry. Anything that we give more power and attention than God is an idol—whether it is a jade Buddha, a false worldview, a person, a body shape, or an idea. Our spin idols need to be exposed and destroyed. In his jealous love, God turns up the heat.

*F*ather of Compassion,

Once again I invite you to help me sort through my emotions. It is one thing to acknowledge my secrets, but quite another for me to answer the call to freedom. That journey confronts my fear and my commitment not to hurt. How shall I choose?

What *am* I afraid of? What will happen to me if I come out of my hiding? What is the worse thing that could happen to me if I tore off my fig leaves and stood naked before you? You assure me that because of Jesus, your gaze is one of welcome and deliverance—not one of shame and humiliation.

Yet I am still afraid. I have little faith at this moment. The risk of moving forward seems fraught with more pain than the pain of staying back. Surely this is not true. The enemy has lied to me long enough. Please increase my faith—for your glory and my salvation.

Jesus, I hear you asking *me,* "Do you want to get well?" I do, I really do. Though I am afraid of the unknown and anxious over what is ahead, I say, "Yes, Jesus, let the healing begin." Quiet my restless heart with your love. Cause me to be silent in the secret places of my heart by your grace. Show me the next step and walk with me hand in hand as you promised Asaph. I take you at your word that you will never leave me or forsake me. I've never needed your presence more. Hear me, Loving Savior, amen.

CHAPTER SEVEN

Your Story of God's Love

My mom had a way of establishing the truth of a matter. With her piercing chocolate-brown eyes, her wry "gotcha" grin, and the "been-there-done-that" expression of a woman who in her *own* childhood was notorious for mischeviousness, she'd look me squarely in the eyes and ask, "Are you telling me a story?"

Whenever she asked that question, Mom wasn't inquiring about my skills as an aspiring storyteller, of which North Carolina has a great tradition. She was hunting for exaggerations, half-truths, and out-and-out lies—all of which I was guilty from time to time.

Story in our home was the equivalent of *tall tale,* and there were no awards for excellence in either. Trust me.

Katherine Hankey had an altogether different concept of *story* in mind when she wrote the beloved hymn "I Love to Tell the Story." This lover of children and daughter of a wealthy English banker is also noted for writing another classic, "Tell Me the Old, Old Story." Both songs were penned during a prolonged illness at the young age of thirty.

For "Kate," *story* meant the remembering and retelling of the great historical events of the life and love of Jesus: his birth, teachings, healing ministry, relationships with people, death, resurrection, second coming—all real elements of a real life. Thus she was moved to write, "I love to tell the story, because I know *'tis true.*" The truthfulness of Jesus' story is the reason we can also sing, "It satisfies my longings, as nothing else can do."

> NO LONGER A FILM CRITIC OR A JUDGE OF CHARACTER, YOU ARE GRABBED BY THE THROAT AS THE MOVIE YELLS, "GOTCHA!"

There are two true stories that need to be brought together if we are to come vibrantly alive to the compelling love of God—Jesus' and our own. For many of us, accessing Jesus' story is easier than getting at our own—and less threatening too. Let's face it, some of us have been telling stories about our story! Foolishly, we prefer fig leaves to the garments of God's grace. Yet the Father continues to ask, "Where are you?"

A WINDOW INTO MY SOUL

My daughter, Kristin, had urged me several times to go see the movie *The Kid.* She wanted us to see it together, but our conflicting schedules postponed our outing for so long that we finally decided I'd go see it without her. For some reason, she *really* wanted me to see that movie. So one Sunday afternoon, Darlene and I went to

Franklin's new twenty-some-screen, digital-sound, high-back-recliner-chair theater (a far cry from the Graham Movie Theater!). Carrying little expectation along with a large box of popcorn and a half-gallon cup of Diet Coke, we found our seats and waded through fifteen minutes of previews. (I still miss the cartoons!)

Forty-seven minutes later, halfway into my bag of salty theater popcorn, equally salty tears were running down my cheeks.

Some movies entertain, others bore, many seduce with promises they cannot deliver, and some anger you over the mindless prattle our culture consumes and celebrates as "great art." But as with a great book, sunset, dream, meal, or song, occasionally a movie comes along that becomes a window into your soul—a means by which your heart is so engaged and then exposed that you feel amazingly moved, vulnerable, and left longing for relief or change.

The line between film and reality gets blurred as your blood pressure starts to rise. Your heart begins to beat faster in response to foolishness, pain, injustice, beauty, or evil played out so believably before your eyes.

Then, all of a sudden—with Nathan-the-prophet-like precision—you see yourself in one of the characters or scenes of the film and *bam!* You realize, "This is *my* story. That's *me. I* am that man!" It's that existential moment of choice when a critical spirit gives way to a convicted heart. No longer a film critic or a judge of character, you are grabbed by the throat as the movie yells, "Gotcha! Now what are ya gonna do?"

As I reached, not for more popcorn, but for another Kleenex from Darlene, I realized why Kristin was so anxious for me to see

this movie. It captured with uncanny accuracy not only the central story line of my life but also the painfully liberating journey I have been on in recent months. I began to feel as if a room full of strangers were watching my home movies or as if I were a cast member in one of those voyeuristic TV shows in which people get voted off the show every week. I hesitated to look around to see who was there, fearing everyone would be looking or pointing at me saying, "That's him, that's him!"

Much like Charles Dickens's classic *A Christmas Carol*, *The Kid* gave me a lens to see my past, present, and possibilities for the future. And my daughter loved me well enough to risk my response.

BIG BARNS AND LITTLE HEARTS

In the movie, Bruce Willis plays an arrogant, self-centered, nearly forty-year-old image consultant. He was oblivious to the man he had become in response to hurtful events of his childhood—including an overbearing and uninvolved father, a severe bout with chubbiness, and the tragic death of his mom when he was about ten.

> HE SHOWS US OUR PAST IN THE LIGHT OF OUR PRESENT TO GIVE US HOPE FOR THE FUTURE.

He is confronted with how poorly he loves by the honesty of a good-hearted, no-nonsense girlfriend and through a disrupting visit from *himself* as a nearly eight-year-old little boy. (Don't try to figure that one out or look for a chapter and verse in the Bible!) The choices he made in response to growing up in a broken family as a broken little boy resulted in his becoming a successful failure. Like the man God calls "fool" in Luke 12, he had big barns and a little heart. Jesus' words, "What does it profit a man to gain the whole world and forfeit his soul?" echoed in my mind through the whole movie.

Through a series of sometimes-humorous, sometimes-painful events, Bruce Willis's character, Rusty, is forced to finally cry uncle. He comes alive to his heretofore forsaken dream of becoming a pilot, having a loving family, and owning a dog named Chester. His buried hurts are unearthed. His proud exterior starts to crumble. His frozen heart begins to thaw.

As the film neared its conclusion, Darlene reached over and took my hand. She didn't need to say a thing. This was one of those times that her touch was enough. All *I* could think to say was *wow*. We left the theater thankful for our daughter's insightfulness and stunned at how timely this movie was.

HELLO, IS ANYBODY LISTENING?

God will not be deterred in getting our attention. He whispers, woos, and warns in myriad ways. Whether he chooses to speak through his Word, his creation, a jackass, a large fish, a whirlwind, a movie, a hard providence, or a friend who dares to love painfully well—God's pursuing heart is everywhere. He shows us our past in the light of our present to give us hope for the future. This is the essence of *story*. " 'For I know the plans I have for you,' declares the LORD, 'plans to prosper you and not to harm you, plans to give you hope and a future' " (Jeremiah 29:11).

The prophet Jeremiah delivered these words of deep encouragement at a time when Israel needed to learn and remember that poor

choices in the past had resulted in the painful circumstances of their present—a connection they should have made by remembering the stories of Israel's previous generations. Essentially Israel was guilty of forsaking the bridal affection of her youth. Other loves were now replacing the love she at first had for her bridegroom (Jeremiah 2:1–2, 5).

SOMETIMES SUFFERING IS THE ONLY MEGAPHONE SUFFICIENT TO GET THE ATTENTION OF OUR UNFAITHFUL AND WANDERING HEARTS.

As humiliating and difficult as the Babylonian captivity was, it was designed by a heart of mercy and it led to certain liberty. Thus Jeremiah proclaimed during the seventy years of captivity, "Because of the LORD's great love we are not consumed, for his compassions never fail. They are new every morning; great is your faithfulness. I say to myself, 'The LORD is my portion; therefore I will wait for him.'… For men are not cast off by the LORD forever. Though he brings grief, he will show compassion, so great is his unfailing love" (Lamentation 3:22–24, 31–32). Sometimes suffering is the only megaphone sufficient to get the attention of our unfaithful and wandering hearts. But there is an easier way!

MIRROR, MIRROR ON THE WALL

The Kid reminded me of why knowing our stories is so very important. Self-awareness is vital to growing in the love of God and in Christlikeness. The Scriptures warn about the man who looks at his face in a mirror then turns away and forgets what he looks like (James 1:24). Indeed, knowing your story is good, but knowing your story in the context of *God's* story is better by far—make that *essential*—for lasting change.

Simon Peter has become for all of us the perfect example of why and how our individual stories must be placed and processed within Jesus' story. Simon the foot-in-mouth-disease apostle; Simon the first-out-of-the-boat

> KNOWING YOUR STORY IS GOOD, BUT KNOWING YOUR STORY IN THE CONTEXT OF *GOD'S* STORY IS BETTER BY FAR.

and "Help-me-Jesus-'cause-I'm-starting-to-sink" disciple; Simon the "Let's-build-three-tabernacles-in-response-to-the-Transfiguration" guy; Simon the ear-cutter-offer; Simon who, much to his shame and brokenness, three times denied that he even knew Jesus on crucifixion eve—it is to this frail and foolish disciple that Jesus gave a personal resurrection appearance (Luke 24:34). What a gift of love and manifestation of grace!

It would be only a short time later when Jesus would remove any lingering doubts about Simon Peter's acceptability. After providing a miraculous catch of fish, Jesus extended to Peter a threefold restoration to counter his threefold denial. "Feed my lambs.... Take care of my sheep.... Feed my sheep!" (John 21:15–19).

DO I REALLY NEED JESUS IN MY STORY?

Knowing your story in the context of God's story eventually leads to the all-important question: *Do I really need Jesus?*

Think for a moment. What if someone came running up to you right now shouting with joy, "You don't have to go to the electric chair! Isn't that great!" How would you respond? Well, it would

probably depend on your context. If you were lying comfortably on a blanket on the beach, you'd respond one way; but if you were sitting in a cell on death row, you'd respond another way.

Or what if a friend came to you in the middle of the night and quietly whispered, "Be still. Don't move. I've got a key to get you out of here. There's a helicopter waiting for us just down the road. We're going home!" Again, how would you respond? If you were a prisoner of war in an enemy camp, your heart would start pounding with joy. But if you were sound asleep in your own bedroom, you'd think your friend was on drugs and would turn over and go back to sleep. Once again, condition determines response.

THE HARD TRUTH IS, WE ARE MUCH WORSE OFF THAN WE THINK.

A siren is heard coming from the distance. As it gets louder you can see the bright red circling light cutting through the encroaching dusk of the evening. The ambulance stops twenty feet from you and a paramedic runs up to you with a filled syringe in hand. "Hold on! We found the antivenom serum. You're gonna be OK!" What's your response this time? Well, if you have the toxins of a poisonous snake coursing through your veins, a sigh of relief and an extended arm are noticeable. But if you are politely sipping a pink lemonade on an after-supper stroll through your neighborhood, you may start wondering if *Candid Camera* is coming back for the twentieth time. Again, depth of need determines desire for cure.

If we don't think we need a savior, we won't look for one beyond ourselves. Jesus came to seek and to save the *lost*, to set *captives* and *prisoners* free, to heal the *sick*. He graciously and powerfully provides forgiveness, freedom, and healing. All of us need all three. The hard truth is, we are much worse off than we think. This is why natural man cannot sustain a graceless gaze upon the face of God. Through God's face, the fullness of his glory shines forth. Proud people like me are tempted to think that we don't need deliverance from God as much as we deserve a break, a few congratulations, and no hassles. Until we take the time to realize how much we need God's transforming love, we will neither seek nor treasure it.

The best way to reflect on our lives is to look into what James 1:25 calls the "perfect law that gives freedom"—the Bible—and to do so in the setting of our relationships. This requires knowing two stories well: God's Word and the record of our relationships—relationships past and present.

Many of us doom ourselves to a life of repeated nonsense and superficiality for a lot of reasons, not the least of which is a refusal to see our stories reflected in the eyes of others all around us. It's one thing to live obsessively for the approval of people and quite another to be appropriately aware of the impact we have on others. God places people in our lives to mirror back to us what we say with our whole being and not just with our careless or well-chosen words.

Until we do this hard and heart work of examining our relationships in the light of God's truth, his love will remain nothing more to us than a philosophical notion, a sentimental feeling, a mere abstraction, or worse, a matter of complete indifference.

REMEMBER YOUR PAST TO GROW YOUR FUTURE

Scientists, sociologists, and psychologists tell us that each of us can be explained primarily in terms of "nature and nurture." We are told that our DNA and experiences in our family of origin pretty well determine who we are. As Christians, however, we know that this is not the whole story of our identity. There is a lot more involved in explaining the human heart than simply focusing on these two profound elements. We are made by God and for God.

King David exclaimed, "You created my inmost being; you knit me together in my mother's womb. I praise you because I am fearfully and wonderfully made.... All the days ordained for me were written in your book before one of them came to be" (Psalm 139:13–14, 16). If we are wrong about our design, we will be wrong about our destiny!

It is an invaluable exercise to remember the significant events in our lives—both the pleasant and unpleasant ones. These can offer helpful insight into understanding who we are. In fact, one of the most repeated commands found throughout the Bible is "Remember." God's people tend to be Cinderella with amnesia: We forget his faithfulness and our foolishness—to our own peril.

But let me hasten to say that the goal of such an inventory is not to make excuses for our wrong choices in life but to gain information that can help explain why we made certain choices. I believe it was Arnold Toynbee, the great historian, who commented that the only thing we learn from history is that we don't learn from history. We are all agents and victims of pain: We have all hurt people we care very deeply about, and likewise, we all carry scars from those who love us. None of us loves or has been loved perfectly. Victimization and vengefulness keep score to get even; wisdom and love remember for the sake of growth and forgiveness.

SEEING THE BIGGER PICTURE

The more we have our eyes opened to see the hand of God at work in one area of our lives, the more we will begin to see his heart at work in other areas, and the clearer the connections between the stories and subplots become. Forrest Gump wasn't entirely wrong to refer to life as a box of chocolates. Surprises do abound! You never know exactly what to expect from the next chapter of life.

And yet as Christians, we have the assurance that life is much more than a series of unrelated surprises. The more time we take to look closely at all the connections in life, the more distinctly we see the meta-narrative of God's grace unfolding.

God has committed not only to finish the "good work" he started in us as individual believers (Philippians 1:6) but also what he has purposed for his whole world. Remember, "For

> WE ARE OBJECTS OF HIS AFFECTION, BUT WE ARE NOT THE POINT OF THE WHOLE STORY!

God so loved the *world* that he gave his one and only Son" (John 3:16, emphasis mine). God loves *what* he has made and *whom* he has made. His love is large enough to fill up heaven with the nations and to fill the nations with heaven.

To grow in grace is to find our place in the larger story of God's love. We are objects of his affection, but we are not the point of the whole story! While the gospel of God's grace is *for* us, it is not *about*

us. To come alive to the compelling love of God is to come alive to the consuming destinations of that love.

As we take, no *make* the time to read the Bible and reflect on our stories through listening, praying, journaling, and good conversation, we begin to see the big picture. It will become clearer to us that *the whole point of the Christian life is to bring glory to God as more and more obstacles to loving well are removed from our hearts.* Let's remind ourselves every day, "The only thing that counts is faith expressing itself through love" (Galatians 5:6).

Nothing is random with our heavenly Father. He is working everything together in our stories to conform to the ultimate purpose of his story (Ephesians 1:11). God is both author and editor. Our lives are not spontaneously thrown together as collections of unrelated short stories. A large story continues to unfold, written before the world began (Psalm 139:16; Ephesians 1:3–6). God is making each of us a living epistle to be read by the watching world—a testimony to his goodness and grace. What is his final purpose? What is his goal? On an individual level, to make us more like Jesus (Romans 8:28–30). And we are never more like Jesus than when we love like Jesus (John 13:34).

Though his ways are not our ways (thankfully), God's plan is perfect and his timing is Swiss.

THE DOMINO EFFECT OF GRACE

Just a couple of weeks after visiting Mom's grave, Pop called to say that he and Ruth, my stepmother, would like to come visit the following weekend. They would drive up Friday and leave Monday. Pop had never stayed at my house for more than twenty-four hours, and now he was going to stay three nights!

Though stunned, I shouldn't have been surprised. Why wouldn't God arrange such a thing? Surely, it was just a matter of time before I would have to confront the one relationship I had avoided more than any other—my relationship with my dad. It was obvious that the Holy Spirit was at work in a most significant way.

As a kid, one of my favorite things to do on boring rainy afternoons was to make a long, intricate design out of dominoes standing end on end. At the strategic moment, I would roll a marble, toy truck, or some other object—fitting the story line of the day—toward the kingpin domino. Then, one by one, each black-and-white-dotted piece would fall under the weight of its cascading neighbor, sending it tumbling into the next. The few seconds it took for everything to be wiped out justified the thirty minutes of setup because I always saw the dominoes as an evil army, opposing team, or dangerous animals.

ONE EXPERIENCE OF GOD'S MERCY LEADS TO THE NEXT.

I have come to think of the Christian life as the "domino effect of grace." As one unloving attitude or selfish habit starts to fall under the weight of grace (and the wait of grace), we can anticipate another will soon begin to topple. One experience of God's mercy leads to the next, as one stronghold of self-preoccupation after another is identified. God is committed to toppling all the obstacles that keep us from loving well.

Not that maturing in the love of God is automatic or easy. Oh, that idols would fall as easily and as quickly as dominoes! Foolishly, like Jonah, we resist the very things that God intends for our growth and freedom. We tend to be just as allergic to seeing our need for God's mercy as we are to extending it to others. As God continued to work in my relationship with Dad, I began to get a clearer picture of what he had in mind for other relationships.

BREAKFAST AT McDONALD'S

Ever since I first started looking at the pictures Moose had brought me, I had wondered what it would be like to look at them with Pop. But how could I "go there" with him? Then I had an idea.

"Darlene," I said tentatively, "when we wake up in the morning, I'm going to take Pop to the Brentwood McDonald's, and if I get my courage up, I'm going to pull out some of Mom's pictures and see if he will talk to me about her."

> POP AND I HAD NEVER HAD A SINGLE CONVERSATION ABOUT MOM, EVEN BEFORE SHE DIED.

Were these words really coming out of my mouth? Pop and I had never had a single conversation about Mom, even before she died. But the work of God's Spirit and the realization that my dad was about to turn eighty-one finally convinced me. "It's not only worth the risk. I have no excuse not to try."

The next morning, Pop and I got in my car and made the five-minute journey to Ronald's land of Happy Meals and Big Macs. I concealed the brown envelope of photos in the morning paper, feeling like a smuggler.

As we had our coffee and biscuits, I simply slid the picture of all four members of our family out onto the tabletop of our booth, the photo in which he is touching my foot.

"Wow, I haven't seen that in a while," Pop said without seeming uncomfortable or surprised at a family picture materializing out of the blue.

"Do you remember where this was taken?" I asked. "Do you recognize the car through the picket fence?" He couldn't recall the specifics, but it was obvious that something had already been stirring in his heart. I now wonder how long he had been waiting for this moment too.

My courage boosted, I pulled out another picture—the one of Mom looking like a calendar girl, sitting on the rocky reef of Carolina Beach. This time he picked up the print and looked carefully. "Now, I do remember taking this picture. We were with friends, and I asked your mom to strike this pose, and it came out so good..." I could see the first tears welling up in his eyes.

"Pop, she had a great smile, didn't she?"

"Oh, yeah, your mom was so outgoing and fun. She never knew a stranger..." Just like that he had moved from giving me a time line and describing the circumstances of a photo to talking about my mom, his beloved wife of only eighteen years.

Next I took out the picture of their wedding day, the one in

which he is in his dress blues and Mom is grinning at him with the gaze of a young lover. "Scott, your mom actually proposed marriage to me. I was so shy, she had to force the issue." He kept looking at the picture taken fifty-seven years earlier. "We got married in Burlington and immediately went to New York, to Brooklyn, for our honeymoon. I had to go to gyrocompass school during the day because I was still in the merchant marines. But for three and a half weeks, we had so much fun going to shows and being together. We saw Louis Armstrong and…" He went on with much animation to tell me stories I wish I could have heard Mom and Dad tell me together. Never, never had I sat with my dad and simply enjoyed a man-to-man, heart-to-heart conversation.

I sat listening and thinking to myself, *Is this really happening? Maybe it's a dream. My dad is not just talking to me about my mom; he is giving me his heart.*

And then, all of a sudden, the most intimate moment I have ever shared with my dad took place. He kept talking as his eyes drank in the memories of Mom with that I've-just-married-you gaze.

"At the end of the class, I had to return to California to get my next ship, and I had to put your mom on the train for Burlington. We were in the Brooklyn train station, and she had to run a quick errand to get some gum or something before leaving. I remember a huge stairwell…"

Pop wasn't storytelling now; he was present in the scene. He looked up as he spoke; he saw my mom. "She stood at the top of the stairs, and I was waiting at the bottom…" Immediately the floodgate of my dad's heart opened, and he started crying the tears of a broken heart. He buried his face in his hands as he wept. Reaching across the table, I started patting him on the shoulder, trying to comfort him in this sacred moment—the kind of moment we had denied ourselves for nearly forty years.

"Scott, I'm sorry. I haven't felt those things in such a long time." Though shaken, he didn't seem at all humiliated or in a hurry to leave McDonald's.

"No, Pop, no. You have nothing to apologize for. You can't imagine what a gift this is to me. To hear you talk about Mom..." I started to lose it. "We both miss her terribly." We sat there silently for another moment, then gathered ourselves and walked to my car. Finally, after sharing life for fifty years as father and son, my dad and I began to connect at a level deeper than sports, politics, and the weather. Our friendship was now in place.

> IT BRINGS GOD GREAT GLORY AND PLEASURE WHEN WE MOVE FROM A PRIVATIZED FAITH TO THE LARGEHEARTEDNESS OF A LIFE OF MERCY AND GENEROSITY IN ALL OF OUR RELATIONSHIPS.

A GREATER PURPOSE

As God began to heal my wounds and change my sinfully self-ish heart, he also began to show me the larger context of this impor-tant work in my life. Learning to express love to my dad is just the beginning. Appropriately grieving my mom's death and getting unstuck relationally are not simply intended to give me a touching

testimony, a good self-image, and freedom to live a safe, comfortable suburban Christian life with a family, a few good friends, and a dog.

It brings God great glory and pleasure when we move from a privatized faith to the largeheartedness of a life of mercy and generosity. A broken water main gets repaired so that liquid refreshment can flow more freely into our homes. A contaminated river in a state park is cleaned of its pollutants so that families and children can once again safely enjoy canoeing, fishing, and swimming. A natural spring is unclogged by the removal of fallen trees and beaver dams so that those downstream will benefit from its beauty and provision. The heart of a Christian gets "unstuck" so that the river of God's grace and mercy can flow through it with greater ease and healing.

We are redeemed to become *conduits,* not merely *receptacles* of God's love and compassion. The river of his affections will not only flow into all of our relationships, but it will also take us into the dark places where poverty, ignorance, racism, oppression, hunger, nakedness, homelessness, and hopelessness thrive—or as the hymn writer has said, "far as the curse is found." It is God's plan to use you and me to give his fallen world a significant taste of what it is going to be like when "no longer will there be any curse" (Revelation 22:3). Indeed, our merciful and mighty Father boldly proclaims, "I am making everything new!" (Revelation 21:5).

This life-giving river will also take us to the nations of the world, for all of history is bound up with God's commitment to redeem sons and daughters unto himself from every single race, tribe, and people group. One day there will be citizens of every nation celebrating citizenship in the Kingdom of God around a throne of grace —all because of the river of God's redemption found in Jesus.

> The four living creatures and the twenty-four elders fell down before the Lamb. Each one had a harp and they were holding golden bowls full of incense, which are the prayers of the saints. And they sang a new song: "You are worthy to take the scroll and to open its seals, because you were slain, and with your blood you purchased men for God from every tribe and language and people and nation. You have made them to be a kingdom and priests to serve our God, and they will reign on the earth." (Revelation 5:8–10)

May such a vision capture our dull and deluded hearts! Certainly this has proven to be a central part of God's fresh work in my heart toward my dad. Gaining a measure of freedom in *that* relationship is indeed just the beginning. As God began to dismantle the idols of self-protection and control in my heart, his river of mercy took me into a land of overwhelming need. We desperately need the power of Jesus to enable us to love well.

Heavenly Father,

Thank you for reminding me of the big story—the unfolding of your redemptive plan for the whole world. It deeply encourages me to know that not only my life but also the entire history of the cosmos is under the control of your loving and powerful hand. You will bring to completion your work in me (I will be made like Jesus.), among the nations of the world (You will redeem your whole family.), and in the

created world itself (You will usher in the new heaven and new earth.). I am filled with hope.

Redeeming Lord, I am also convicted as I keep this big picture in view, for I know that I am selfish and self-centered. Help me accept and rejoice in the fact that I am not the point of the whole story. I matter deeply to you, but I am not all that matters! Remind me of this when I fall into self-pity or walk about with an exaggerated notion of my importance.

As the old and true story of Jesus and his love continues to intersect with my story of brokenness, weakness, and sin, may new chapters of redemption and love be written upon my heart and through my life. Who are you calling me to love that I am avoiding? I need your strength and grace to help me connect with friends and family alike.

And please give me what you command—a love for the poor, the alien, the widows and orphans. Free me from racism in all its forms. Make me a merciful warrior of justice, righteousness, and peace. Burden my heart with the joy of taking the gospel to the nations of the world. Change me, free me, and focus me for your glory. Amen.

No discipline seems *pleasant* at the time,
but PAINFUL.
Later on, however,
it produces a harvest of *righteousness*
and PEACE for those
who have been *trained* by it.
—Hebrews 12:11

God moves in a *mysterious* way,
His wonders to perform;
He plants His *footsteps* in the sea,
And rides upon the storm.
Ye fearful saints, fresh *courage* take,
The clouds ye so much dread
Are big with *mercy,* and shall break
In blessings on your head.

William Cowper (1731–1800)

CHAPTER EIGHT

The Love of Suffering

W hy, Scotty, why?" Tears streamed down Steven's face as we broke bread together over his broken heart. "Why of all people in South Africa would God take my brother? You don't understand; you just don't understand!" he said, almost shouting. "Trevor was the most amazing person I ever knew, and I'm not saying that because he was my brother. The Kingdom of God needs him in Cape Town.

"When Trevor was given a full-year fellowship to do AIDS research at Harvard, he stayed only four months because of his concern for his friends and family back home. I remember his calling several times from Boston just to counsel and encourage one of his friends who was battling alcoholism. He was such a lover of people—so gentle, so kind. He drove a simple car, wore simple clothes, but his heart was *so* big. I will never forget him telling me to

go across the fellowship hall at church to welcome a stranger in our midst. That's the kind of person he was. He always sought out the struggling students in his classes to serve them any way he could."

I had just finished my first couple of lectures on the topic of suffering for a group of about fifty pastors and laymen gathered at a "colored" church in Cape Town, South Africa. Steven and I were having lunch and moving my talks from the realm of the abstract into the visceral region of real life. Just four weeks earlier Steven had buried his cancer-stricken older brother. He was devastated not just by the personal loss, but by what seemed to be a cruel act of God toward his people in South Africa.

"I CANNOT UNDERSTAND WHY GOD TOOK HIM."

Over the course of the next two days, I met with Trevor's widow, Jenni, and her four beautiful daughters, Gwyneth, Megan, Terri-Sue, and Amy-Lee. I also had fellowship with a group of elders from their church who were struggling to make sense of this hard piece of providence. The same question spilled from each heart: "Why would a God of love allow us who have suffered so much to suffer still more?"

One of the brothers, also a physician with a doctorate from Oxford University, spoke with biting pain. "Scotty, there were twenty-five hundred people at Trevor's funeral, pretty much equally divided between Jews, Christians, and Muslims. There was no one—regardless of race, religion, economics, or politics—who didn't feel warmly accepted by him. Many of those present had come to faith as a result of Trevor's life and witness. Others were deeply saddened by the loss of a man who was one of the world's emerging experts on AIDS—the disease that is devastating our country. He was in a position to help so many." He paused, then said, "I cannot understand why God took him."

Another of the elders revealed his love and his anguish: "What do we say to our children at church? We have taught them that they can trust God in all things and for all things. We all prayed and fasted for God to heal Trevor. What is this going to do to our children's faith?"

By God's grace, I wept with these men rather than trying to teach them. Though I had "answers" to give them from the Scriptures, my words would have been not so much irrelevant as irreverent in that sacred moment. Though their sentences seemed to end with question marks, they were really punctuated with exclamation points. These elders did not need my theology as much as they needed my ears and heart. There would be an appropriate time for us to examine the Scriptures together, but this wasn't it. Jesus has much to teach all of us about weeping with those who weep.

But Trevor's story proved to be just the beginning.

PLEASE PRAY FOR MY DAUGHTER

Having given the last of my messages for the two-day conference, I felt encouraged to invite any of the attendees to come up afterward for prayer. Though I am quite accustomed to praying with individuals at the end of one of our church services in Tennessee, the prayer requests of these pastors and lay leaders were hard to imagine and absorb. Their requests came out of stories of poverty, persecution, murder, and demonic activity—not the usual needs that are

whispered into my ear at the front of our worship center in Franklin. But one gentle lady in particular is burned into my memory from that day. I hope, forever.

"Pastor, would you please pray for my daughter?" she began. "She is eleven and has been raped. Men with AIDS in our community have been taught a devilish superstition. They believe they can rid themselves of the disease if they have sex with a virgin girl before her twelfth birthday. Just such a man took my daughter. Please pray that she hasn't been infected with AIDS and pray for her heart. She is so frightened. Pray for me as well, that I will know how to care for her and that I will be able to forgive the bad man that did this horrible deed."

Literally, my knees buckled. How can we comprehend something so evil, so "devilish"? I prayed with my sister the best I knew how. But it was she who needed to pray for me. The very fact that she wanted God to give her grace to forgive her daughter's rapist revealed a profound grasp of the gospel and a knowledge of the heart of God that left my unmerciful heart very convicted.

How Can a Loving God…?

How can a loving, involved, and almighty God and Father allow his sons and daughters to suffer cruelties like the death by cancer of great leaders like Trevor or the rape of eleven-year-old little girls? And why did my mom have to die in a stupid car wreck?

Where was the God who delights in, sings over, and quiets his people with love? How can we take the words "never again will you fear any harm" seriously? How can God be with us and "mighty to save" (Zephaniah 3:15, 17) when we continue to experience great pains—physically, emotionally, spiritually, and mentally? How can we reconcile the claim that we are the objects of God's affection with the reality of human suffering?

A NEW PERSPECTIVE

Close to downtown Cape Town, reaching thousands of feet above ground level, is Table Mountain, one of the most popular tourist attractions in the area. This volcanic extrusion looks like a gigantic tabletop that has been strategically placed in the middle of the city. After a cable-car ride to the top, visitors can spend hours walking around the notoriously flat surface of this large mountain and gain a perspective on the life of Cape Town from every direction—a perspective that cannot be appreciated by those who live in the lowlands, hugging the paths of daily life.

> HOW CAN WE RECONCILE THE CLAIM THAT WE ARE THE OBJECTS OF GOD'S AFFECTION WITH THE REALITY OF HUMAN SUFFERING?

It is just such a perspective that we need when we ask the question *Why? Why does a loving God allow so much suffering?* If we live only on the road of great pain, such a question appears to have no satisfactory answers. We desperately need to see suffering, like everything else, from God's vantage point.

The apostle John wrote the book of Revelation during a time of incredible suffering for the people of God. As he wrote, John himself —perhaps eighty years old—was in exile, a prisoner of Rome, living in a rocky penal colony on the island of Patmos. He wrote to encourage

God's people in the midst of the horrors of persecution, suffering, and martyrdom. Satan was intent on destroying Christianity and Christians—either by persecution, seduction, or the perversion of truth through false teaching.

THE PEOPLE OF GOD CONSISTENTLY CRY OUT FOR RELIEF, AND THE GOD OF LOVE BIDS US TRUST HIM.

Early in Revelation, John records one of many visions God gave him in order to comfort the troubled hearts of Christians living through the first massive wave of persecutions directed against Jesus' bride. "After this I looked, and there before me was a door standing open in heaven. And the voice I had first heard speaking to me like a trumpet said, 'Come up here, and I will show you what must take place after this'" (Revelation 4:1). We need what John was given:

1. God's gracious invitation to ponder the difficult things *with* him ("come up here")

2. *his* trustworthy interpretation on suffering (*"I* will show you")

3. the assurance that there is meaning to pain and that God is in control ("what *must* take place after this")

We have all three of these in the Bible.

CONTEXT IS CRITICAL

Interestingly enough, the most-asked question in the whole Bible—from Genesis to Revelation—is "How long, O Lord, how long?" And the most repeated command from God is "Do not fear" or "Do not be afraid." The people of God consistently cry out for relief, and the God of love bids us trust him. When we listen, what does he speak to us about suffering? What do the Scriptures teach us about the reason, purpose, duration, and end of suffering? First of all, we learn the importance of context.

We all know the effect of walking into a movie forty minutes late. You are likely to be bored, disturbed, confused, or thrilled by the first scene you encounter. But apart from the *whole* story, it is impossible to fully understand the meaning of one part of the movie. Context is critical to everything. And suffering has a very distinctive context in the unfolding, progressive revelation of God's Word. The entire story line of the Bible consists of four parts:

1. Creation

2. Fall

3. Redemption

4. Consummation

Each of these four must be understood as a part of a whole narrative that God is writing. To forget even one of them will distort not only how we view the mystery of pain, evil, and suffering but also how we think about God himself.

ONE OF THE REASONS THAT SUFFERING IS SO UNACCEPTABLE TO OUR HEARTS IS THAT WE ARE NOSTALGIC FOR EDEN.

Creation: God created a perfect world in which he placed his first son and daughter, Adam and Eve. There was no evil, pain, suffering, or brokenness. Everything was good, true, and beautiful in Eden. In fact, one of the reasons that suffering is so unacceptable to our hearts is that we are nostalgic for Eden. Our

DNA cries out that something is terribly wrong with a world in which everything is broken.

Fall: Through Adam and Eve's willful act of rebellion against the God of perfect love, sin was introduced into the human heart and the whole world. When Adam and Eve partook of the forbidden fruit from the tree of the knowledge of good and evil, God proved he was not a liar. He warned our first parents of the price of violating his amazing covenant of love. When they died spiritually, they brought the consequences of his judgment into *everything*. The entire cosmos is now infected with sin, decay, death, and frustration as a result of their sin and the corresponding curse God placed upon the world.

Indeed, we live in a *very* fallen world. Nothing is as bad as it could be because of God's restraining grace, but nothing is as good as it was meant to be because the pollution of sin affects everything and everyone. Suffering, in all its expressions, is one of the clearest and loudest demonstrations of the fallen state of the world.

Redemption: But God, who is rich in mercy, love, and grace, has also chosen to reveal himself as Redeemer. He has taken upon himself the task, joy, and cost of reconciling a people unto himself and of re-creating all things in their Edenic glory. The whole Bible, from Genesis 3:15 through Revelation 22:21, is the chronicling of this story of redemption.

This magnificent work of re-creation and restoration is accomplished through the gift of God's Son, Jesus. It is Jesus who has "crushed the head of the serpent" by his death upon the cross. It is only by his sufferings that all suffering of the people of God will one day be done away with. The great story line of redemption is unfolding all around us, but it will only be complete on that final day.

Consummation: A day has been set when Jesus will return to bring to completion all that the Father has begun. Then a "new heaven and a new earth" will be ushered in—far more glorious than Eden! It will be more glorious because of its international scope: Men and women from every nation will inhabit this new world, as opposed to the one man and one woman who inhabited Eden. It will be more glorious because, unlike Eden, the possibility of sin, even temptation, will never exist again! Adam and Eve were only innocent before the Fall; we have been made perfectly righteous like Jesus—and will remain so forever. It will also be more glorious because God will be worshiped as Creator *and* Redeemer—forever!

> ADAM AND EVE WERE ONLY INNOCENT BEFORE THE FALL; WE HAVE BEEN MADE PERFECTLY RIGHTEOUS LIKE JESUS.

Then, and only then, will God "wipe every tear from their eyes. There will be no more death or mourning or crying or pain, for the old order of things has passed away" (Revelation 21:4).

The apostle John got this vision from atop a heavenly "Table Mountain." God showed him the big picture so that the little pictures, including those of suffering, would be seen in context. This is the same eternal perspective that moved Paul—a man who endured more than any I have known (2 Corinthians 11:22–33)—to write,

> I consider that our present sufferings are not worth comparing with the glory that will be revealed in us. The creation waits in eager expectation for the sons of God to be revealed.

For the creation was subjected to frustration, not by its own choice, but by the will of the one who subjected it, in hope that the creation itself will be liberated from its bondage to decay and brought into the glorious freedom of the children of God.

We know that the whole creation has been groaning as in the pains of childbirth right up to the present time. Not only so, but we ourselves, who have the firstfruits of the Spirit, groan inwardly as we wait eagerly for our adoption as sons, the redemption of our bodies. For in this hope we were saved. (Romans 8:18–24)

We will suffer as long as we live in this fallen world. But there is another world coming!

BUT WHY DOES GOD ALLOW SUFFERING?

In addition to the "context" of suffering, God's Word provides us with more answers still. Although understanding the *whys* of suffering does not decrease the intensity of the pain, it does give us a much-needed new perspective.

Some are persecuted for righteousness' sake. Thirteen hundred people filled the room that cold July 1993 evening at the worship center of St. James Church in Kenilworth, one of the many neighborhoods in the beautiful port city of Cape Town, South Africa. The music had already begun when the men burst in through the church door just to the left of the stage. Dressed in dark clothing, one of them was carrying some type of a gun—bigger than a pistol but smaller than a rifle. At first, none of the worshipers knew what to make of the abrupt interruption. The Sunday evening service was outreach oriented and attracted a broad range of people from the community. Was this a planned drama staged by the youth group to set the context for the evening message?

All uncertainty was removed as the first gunman indiscriminately opened fire on the congregation with an R4 automatic weapon. The horrifying sound of shots and screams shattered the joy and peace always shared in that room—and also in the lives of the gathered Christians. In shock, they dove for whatever cover they could find, hoping the barrage of bullets would soon be over.

DURING THE TWENTIETH CENTURY MORE CHRISTIANS DIED AS MARTYRS THAN THE COMBINED NUMBER OF THE PRECEDING NINETEEN CENTURIES.

But then, one of the assailants threw a hand grenade attached to a can of nails into one section of pews. The sound made by the explosion was forever burned into the ears of the survivors, including my friend Larry Warren, who was present that night.

This tragic story is just one of many in which believers experience great pain and sorrow for no other reason than because they belong to Jesus. In fact, during the twentieth century more Christians died as martyrs than the combined number of the preceding nineteen centuries. It is estimated that with the beginning of the twenty-first century, two hundred million Christians are experiencing various degrees of persecution every day.

Is such treatment contradictory of the love of God? Consider Jesus' words:

> Blessed are those who are persecuted because of righteousness, for theirs is the kingdom of heaven. Blessed are you when

people insult you, persecute you and falsely say all kinds of evil against you because of me. Rejoice and be glad, because great is your reward in heaven, for in the same way they persecuted the prophets who were before you. (Matthew 5:10–12)

How did the early church respond to this type of suffering? One day after being flogged by the members of the religious establishment for openly proclaiming that Jesus is the Messiah, "The apostles left the Sanhedrin, rejoicing because they had been counted worthy of suffering disgrace for the Name. Day after day, in the temple courts and from house to house, they never stopped teaching and proclaiming the good news that Jesus is the Christ" (Acts 5:41–42).

Some suffer the painful consequences

> SUCH SUFFERING MAY BE TRAGIC, BUT IT IS NOT POINTLESS.

of their sin. Sometimes we suffer for no other reason than that we are *stupid!* Peter writes, "If you suffer, it should not be as a murderer or thief or any other kind of criminal, or even as a meddler. However, if you suffer as a Christian, do not be ashamed, but praise God that you bear that name" (1 Peter 4:15–16).

We can bring great pain upon ourselves if we go beyond what God says we are free to do as his sons and daughters. I cannot blame God if all my friends leave me because I cannot resist meddling in their private affairs. That is suffering for being a nuisance, not for being a Christian. If I lose my driver's license and have to pay a two hundred dollar fine for going eighty-five in a thirty-five–mile-per-hour zone, I suffer as a moron, not as a martyr!

God warns and woos our hearts before final judgment. If man is designed for rich and deeply satisfying relationship with God, isn't it a sign of his love, rather than his disdain or indifference, when he uses whatever means of drawing us to himself? Paul writes, "The wrath of God is being revealed from heaven against all the godlessness and wickedness of men who suppress the truth by their wickedness" (Romans 1:18). Better small portions (even large ones!) of great discomfort now than to suffer the eternal consequences of our sins. Such suffering may be tragic, but it is not pointless.

When God is severe and when he is forbearing, his goal is the same. "Do you show contempt for the riches of his kindness, tolerance and patience, not realizing that God's kindness leads you toward repentance?" (Romans 2:4). God whispers in our comforts, and he shouts in our adversities.

Our Father disciplines us in love. I never enjoyed getting the "belt" as a kid. Mom was always within bounds, however, whenever she had to resort to such measures. I remember only a half-dozen or so times when I perceived the sizzling sting of leather through my pants on my sitting apparatus. But the prepunishment spiel and routine was always the same. "This is going to hurt me more than it does you."

After four or five wince-producing pops, Mom would *try* to hug me. But I didn't feel like a hug after being disciplined. In fact, I wanted a different mother at the moment! But an hour or so later, I wanted her touch very much. I knew she was right.

The author of Hebrews represents the disciplining love of God in a similar fashion:

Endure hardship as discipline; God is treating you as sons. For what son is not disciplined by his father? If you are not

disciplined (and everyone undergoes discipline), then you are illegitimate children and not true sons. Moreover, we have all had human fathers who disciplined us and we respected them for it. How much more should we submit to the Father of our spirits and live! Our fathers disciplined us for a little while as they thought best; but God disciplines us for our good, that we may share in his holiness. No discipline seems pleasant at the time, but painful. Later on, however, it produces a harvest of righteousness and peace for those who have been trained by it. (Hebrews 12:7–11)

God can be both light and quite severe in this discipline of love. He may withhold his presence, or he may bring some great and prolonged difficulty into our lives. But the goal is the same: As our Father, he is determined that we share the family likeness. Thus, such discipline is best seen as correction rather than punishment. Jesus has already been fully punished for all of our sins—past, present, and future. But to go from looking like orphans of sin to sons and daughters of the living God—well, that's a piece of work! Allow me a personal and painful example.

> AS OUR FATHER, HE IS DETERMINED THAT WE SHARE THE FAMILY LIKENESS.

Right after performing my daughter's wedding I had braces put on my teeth. This wasn't cruel and unusual punishment for a forty-eight-year-old man; it was correction. My front teeth were growing more crossed and outward as I got older. I was biting my lower lip whenever I ate.

The braces, though painful, corrected the problem. Likewise, we often need orthodontics of the heart. And when we do, God's fatherly discipline comes to the rescue! He is committed to replacing our hearts of stone with hearts of flesh. Such a transformation requires a ton of correction! Brace yourselves! One day, not merely your smile but your heart will be like that of Jesus.

Some suffer to fulfill the hidden purposes of God. Some explanations for suffering will remain veiled to us until we are in heaven. Paul implied as much when he wrote, "Now we see but a poor reflection as in a mirror; then we shall see face to face. Now I know in part; then I shall know fully, even as I am fully known" (1 Corinthians 13:12). Though it is frustrating, even at times maddening, not to have all the answers *now*, it is a wonderful gift to be guaranteed that one day we will get closure. It is in this hope-filled category that I have camped out and continue to process the tragedy of my mom's death when I was eleven.

The story of Job is a great example of how our loving Father sometimes chooses not to let us in on the reasons and meaning of great reversals and torment. Job is identified as "blameless and upright," a man who "feared God and shunned evil" (Job 1:1). God blessed him with a large family, a huge estate, and great wealth. Job kind of reminds me of Ben Cartwright, the wise father on the old TV show *Bonanza!* (Most of you are too young to remember Ben. What a shame!)

One day, a conversation took place in heaven between God and Satan that Job knew nothing about. But it was a dialogue that would forever affect his life. Satan basically charged God with being a "sugar daddy."

In essence, Satan said, "The only reason your people love you is that you have bought their affection. Take away Job's good life, and he will curse you to your face" (Job 1:6–11).

Though God didn't need to prove anything to anyone, he gave Satan permission to destroy Job's family, estate, and wealth (Job 1:12–19). Soon after that, permission was granted to destroy his health (Job 2:4–8). Are you already asking *why?* Imagine *Job's* confusion, then anguish, and then cosmic questioning.

> SATAN BASICALLY CHARGED GOD WITH BEING A "SUGAR DADDY."

Over the course of the next season of life, Job's wife grew disgusted with his faith, "Are you still holding on to your integrity? Curse God and die!" (Job 2:9), and with his breath, "My breath is offensive to my wife" (Job 19:17). Talk about an encouraging wife! He also enjoyed the benefit of having his friends take turns at blaming and shaming him.

Now, most of us know how the story ends. God shows up, big-time (Job 38–41). He reveals his majesty to Job, and he gives his son a new family, estate, and wealth—with great health until he reached his 140th birthday! (Job 42:12–17). (Do not think for a moment that ten new children erased the pain and memory of the ten who died.)

But nowhere did God answer Job's entire list of "why" questions. There is nothing in the text that implies that God ever told Job, in this life, about that little conversation in heaven. The purpose behind Job's losses and torment remained quite hidden. Think about it: What if Job had been given a private briefing by God about what was going on? What a different perspective Job would have had!

But our loving God chose to remain an inscrutable God. Somewhere in our hearts we have to hear and accept God saying, "My thoughts are not your thoughts, neither are your ways my ways.... As the heavens are higher than the earth, so are my ways higher than your ways and my thoughts than your thoughts" (Isaiah 55:8–9). If we think that God's love and his lack of revelation are mutually exclusive, then it is *we* who confirm Satan's charge. We are the ones looking for a "sugar daddy."

Sometimes we suffer to accomplish a greater good. Though we must be careful to guard against the notion that every painful event has a tit-for-tat purpose in life, it is consistent with the gospel to ask, "How might God use this horrible event, situation, even evil, to accomplish a greater good?"

The story of Joseph is a classic example of this way of responding to hard providences. Genesis, the "book of beginnings," ends with the magnificent story of a new beginning for the people of God in Egypt (Genesis 37–50).

Joseph, Jacob's most-loved son, was a major irritation to his older brothers. Whether it was his dreams of prominence among his siblings or his multicolored robe shouting that he was Papa's favorite, Joseph's brothers had had enough. Initially, they planned to kill him and throw his body into an empty water cistern in the desert. But Reuben's warning and Judah's reasoning led the brothers to sell Joseph for eight ounces of silver to a caravan of Midianite merchants. Joseph was taken to Egypt and separated from his family for twenty years.

During those years, Joseph went from the penthouse to the outhouse and back to the penthouse. His stint in the home and graces of Potiphar, captain of Pharaoh's guard, was cut short because he spurned the sexual advances of Potiphar's wife. He was sent to prison for more than a decade for the crime of not sleeping around. While in prison, his visionary gift enabled him to interpret the dreams of two fellow inmates—the king's cupbearer and baker. Joseph's reputation of being good with dreams spread to the Pharaoh. None of Pharaoh's magicians, counselors, or wise men could interpret his dreams.

Enter Joseph, not only into Pharaoh's chamber, but also into his service. Joseph was put in charge of the whole land of Egypt, being second in command only to Pharaoh.

As revealed in Pharaoh's dreams, seven good years of harvest gave way to seven lean years of famine. Their father, Jacob, sent Joseph's brothers to Egypt to buy grain so the family could survive. Through the course of events, Joseph had a dramatic reunion with them. How would

IF ANYONE EVER SUFFERED FAMILIAL ABUSE, IT WAS HE.

he respond? With spite and bitterness? If anyone ever came from a dysfunctional family, it was Joseph. If anyone ever suffered familial abuse, it was he. Joseph's brothers certainly feared his response after all those years. "What if Joseph holds a grudge against us and pays us back for all the wrongs we did to him?" (Genesis 50:15).

> His brothers then came and threw themselves down before him. "We are your slaves," they said. But Joseph said to them, "Don't be afraid. Am I in the place of God? You intended to

harm me, but God intended it for good to accomplish what is now being done, the saving of many lives. So then, don't be afraid. I will provide for you and your children." And he reassured them and spoke kindly to them. (Genesis 50:18–21)

WHAT WE LEARN FROM JOSEPH'S SUFFERING

I do not assume that Joseph came to this amazing healing and theological conviction easily. We would do harm to the integrity and consistent testimony of Scripture to overly spiritualize Joseph's journey, as though he never wrestled with doubt, anger, or unbelief. But whatever his struggle with the ways of God during those twenty years, Joseph's experience of suffering and love have left us a timeless and prophetic model.

We dare not put ourselves in God's place. He alone has the right to exact judgment. Joseph's question is profound: "Am I in the place of God?" When we look carefully and honestly at the circumstances, isn't it the case, more often than not, that our railings against suffering and injustice are man-centered rather than God-centered?

Suffering evil at the hands of men can be a means of accomplishing the good of God. "What you meant for evil God meant for good." You want a mystery and paradox to ponder until Jesus comes back? Try this one: Though God condemns the sin of Joseph's brothers, he used it—no, the text is stronger—he *meant* it for good. At this point we are driven to see Joseph and his experience as a profound type pointing to the greater Joseph who would suffer the greatest wickedness imaginable at the hands of men and Satan. Consider how God tells this part of the story.

"Men of Israel, listen to this: Jesus of Nazareth was a man

accredited by God to you by miracles, wonders and signs, which God did among you through him, as you yourselves know. This man was handed over to you by God's set purpose and foreknowledge; and you, with the help of wicked men, put him to death by nailing him to the cross" (Acts 2:22–23).

Those who crucified Jesus are both guilty of murder and agents of providence. This is a sovereign and glorious mystery. Though God cannot be charged with evil, he orchestrates and uses (redeems) "the legends of the fall" to accomplish the purposes of heaven.

To desire the saving of many lives over the preservation of one's own life is the way of the cross. It is the "saving of many lives" that defines Jesus' suffering. And to a lesser, but still most meaningful, sense, ours. As Jesus hung upon the cross—beaten, naked, and shamed—"Those who passed by hurled insults at him, shaking their heads and saying,

> THOUGH GOD CANNOT BE CHARGED WITH EVIL, HE ORCHESTRATES AND USES (REDEEMS) "THE LEGENDS OF THE FALL" TO ACCOMPLISH THE PURPOSES OF HEAVEN.

'You who are going to destroy the temple and build it in three days, save yourself! Come down from the cross, if you are the Son of God!'" (Matthew 27:39–40).

What if he had come down from the cross? What would have been the effect? He would have saved himself, but he could not have saved us. It was either one or the other. Precisely because he was and is the Son of God, Jesus stayed on the cross, *abandoned by God,* so that we can be *delighted in by God.* When an angel of the Lord told another Joseph of the divine conception of Jesus in Mary's womb by the Holy Spirit, he proclaimed with holy joy, "You are to give him the name Jesus, because he will save his people from their sins" (Matthew 1:21). Jesus has come to save us from the guilt of our sins and from every effect of sin occasioned by the Fall. He forgives, redeems, and heals; and he is making all things new—for all who trust in Him.

It is the suffering of Jesus that answers our cry for justice in the face of evil, suffering, and injustice. And it is the suffering Jesus who knows how to console us until the promised day of vindication and consummation of our redemption. With our twin cry for justice and love, let us continue to survey the wondrous cross upon which the Prince of Glory died. There is no greater love.

How Then Shall We Live?

How then shall we live in view of Jesus' suffering for others and for us? First, we must live in profound adoration and gratitude. "For Christ died for sins once for all, the righteous for the unrighteous, to bring you to God" (1 Peter 3:18). His cross has brought us into the Father's embrace.

But second, our lives must be an intentional surrender to a life defined by the sufferings of the cross. "To this you were called, because Christ suffered for you, leaving you an example, that you should follow in his steps" (1 Peter 2:21). To take up our own cross daily is to identify with the other-centered love of Jesus. It is to willingly and gladly embrace the high cost of suffering love as the purest expression of our calling to be "living sacrifices." There is no greater worship we can offer the God to whom we are *objects of his affection.*

Wonderful, Merciful Savior,

I begin by praising you for your suffering on my behalf. As I spend more time surveying your wondrous cross, I marvel at such astounding love, and I am also confronted, once again, by my unbelief. Jesus, by the power of your Spirit, cause my heart to more fully grasp that you were betrayed, despised, rejected, beaten, mocked, and crucified for *me*. May your cross increasingly have a redemptively disturbing presence and a transforming power in my heart. Love so amazing, so divine, demands my life, my soul, my all.

Father, may the suffering of your Son help me understand all the evil, injustice, and tragedies that permeate history and abound in the world of which I am a part. When I am tempted to doubt your goodness, power, and wisdom in the face of so much pain and darkness, I will look to Jesus and say, "This is how much my God hates evil. This is his response to manifold wickedness and pain. He has caused his Son to suffer as none other so that one day all suffering will be eradicated!" I worship you with passionate awe.

Jesus, as you are so familiar with suffering and grief, give me your heart to care tenderly and patiently for the hurting ones in my life. Help me to be more committed to love than to fix, more ready to listen than to give answers, more prepared to stay present than to run away in the face of so much brokenness. I choose to live in light of the day when there will be no more suffering, pain, and evil. Even so, Lord Jesus, come quickly. Until then I cling to you, Precious Redeemer and Friend. Amen.

I WILL GIVE THEM
AN UNDIVIDED *heart*
AND PUT A NEW SPIRIT IN THEM;
I WILL REMOVE FROM THEM
THEIR *heart* OF STONE
AND GIVE THEM A HEART OF FLESH.
—EZEKIEL 11:19

Jesus, the very thought of Thee
With *sweetness* fill my breast
But sweeter for Thy face to see
And in Thy *presence* rest
Our restless spirits yearn for Thee
Wherever our changeful lot is cast
Glad when Thy *gracious smile* we see
Blest when our faith can hold Thee fast.

*B*ernard of Clairvaux (c. 1150)

CHAPTER NINE

Obstacles to Intimacy

If it's true that we are, indeed, the objects of our Creator's affection, why do so many of us feel estranged and distant from the Lover of our souls? Why does our relationship with our Pursuer lack intimacy and depth?

There are as many different answers to these questions as there are disconnected believers. But let's look at a few of the most common. See if you can't find yourself reflected in some of these obstacles to intimacy.

OBSTACLE #1: FAILURES AND DETOURS IN THE HEALING JOURNEY OF GRIEF

Though all of us experience various forms of suffering in life, many of us carry the raw fury of emotional pain and loss decades after the event(s) that wounded our souls. Such open wounds challenge

our ability to trust and rest in the goodness of God. Certainly, my story makes this observation more than theory for me. But I am not alone. As a pastor I have counseled and prayed with hundreds of men and women whose unhealed (and in many cases, unacknowledged) abuse, betrayals, and tragedies have seemingly mocked any hope of intimacy with God.

The answer? Taking the road far less traveled—the healing journey of grief. I continue to reflect on Dan Allender's words: "Scotty, two things define you more than the love of God—your busy, noisy spirit and your failure to grieve your mom's death."

The connection between grieving my mom's death, knowing my heavenly Father more intimately, and relating deeply with my dad and others has become increasingly obvious. The more time and emotional energy we invest in appropriately grieving our losses before the Lord, the greater the probability that we will experience his healing presence and caring heart. I so wish I had started the journey of grief much sooner in life—if not as a young adolescent, then at least when Dan boldly confronted me when I was thirty-three.

> THE MORE TIME AND EMOTIONAL ENERGY WE INVEST IN APPROPRIATELY GRIEVING OUR LOSSES BEFORE THE LORD, THE GREATER THE PROBABILITY THAT WE WILL EXPERIENCE HIS HEALING PRESENCE AND CARING HEART.

What is the shape of "normal" grief? The apostle Paul affirms that Christians do indeed grieve, but not as those "who have no hope" (1 Thessalonians 4:13). What, then, is "good grief"? Though I hesitate to offer what might be viewed as a definitive guide to grieving well, allow me to at least suggest several aspects of the process that are common to most of us.

Each story and heart is different. The path to healing will take on a different look for each of us. As you read the following, try to think of your own stories of loss and how you have responded through the years. Perhaps my reluctant and fitful jour-ney along this liberating but demand-ing path will help you identify some detours you have taken. Think also about how you have responded to others in their grief.

> WE MUST BE VERY CAREFUL ABOUT DEFINING WHAT "DOING WELL" MEANS.

Shock, Denial, and Numbness. In the first moments after a great trauma or loss, many people immediately fall apart. It is not unusual for a loved one to faint, scream, or weep uncontrollably under the weight of the devastating news. Others seem to do "amazingly well"—whether through natural endomorphines, supernatural grace, or denial mechanisms. Both of these responses are quite pre-dictable and normal. But as we deal with grief in our own lives or care for someone who has suffered a crisis, we must be very careful about defining what "doing well" means. We must resist the tempta-tion of setting up a standard that we or another grieving person has to live up to. "You were doing so well; what happened?"

Personally, I went straight into denial. I simply refused to accept that Mom was dead. "Falling apart" would have been "doing well" for me, but I had no context to do so other than burying my face in a pillow. Our home became a house in which a dad and his two sons were paralyzed and isolated from one another. Every man and boy

for himself. It would have been wonderful to have had a community—people present, but not pushy—mentors in grief, but not "fixers."

Disorientation. After the initial experience of shock or denial, a season of disorientation sets in. Try to imagine what an amputee experiences after waking up from surgery to the startling realization that a leg has been removed from his body. How does one resume "daily routines" with one leg? Understandably, amputees go through a painful and prolonged time of discovering the gravity of loss. How does one learn to walk again? The death of someone we love—especially the death of a spouse, parent, or child—is an amputation of the soul. The degree of disorientation is essentially determined by the importance and quality of the relationship.

> IT IS ONLY IN THE PRESENCE OF GOD AND COMMUNITY THAT WE CAN BEGIN TO FIND OUR BEARINGS AND REGAIN A SENSE OF PERSPECTIVE AND BALANCE.

Losing my mom was like an amputation of my whole being. She was the nerve center, heart, limbs, and life of our world. Our family believed in God, but we believed in Mom a little more. As Dad later said on a tape recording he made for me of the history of his relationship with Mom, "When Martha died, the life went out of all of us." How true. I am only now beginning to understand the gravity of my loss, thirty-nine years later. Once again, it is only in the presence of God and community that we can begin to find our bearings and regain a sense of perspective and balance.

Volatile Emotions. As the process of grief takes hold, it's not unusual for feelings of deep anger, anguish, and resentment to take over for a season. "Why me? Why now? Why, why, WHY!" The anger of grief is more closely related to hurt than to what may appear to be "meanspiritedness." When something or someone precious is taken from you, it's *supposed* to hurt, and anger is an appropriate response. The record of Jesus' agonizing tears shed at the death of his friend Lazarus forever speak well of the heartrending pain experienced by those who love well. "Jesus wept. Then the Jews said, 'See how he loved him!'" (John 11:35–36).

In my story, there was no observable anger or extreme emotion. Anger is an emotion I have resisted all of my life—at least obvious forms of it, such as outbursts, screaming, and breaking stuff. At eleven years old I was clueless about my emotions, and I was so frightened when I heard my dad wailing in grief late at night. I remember simply wanting to be happy again.

I now realize how important it is for us as parents to learn how to nurture the emotional lives of our children. We can do so only as we ourselves are growing emotionally. Be encouraged. As my dad and I have been coming alive emotionally in our relationship, the fruit of this movement is spilling over into my relationships with my wife and children. More dominoes of grace.

Guilt. "What more could I have done?" is a question that gets asked after a great loss. "I wish I'd been able to _____." Memories of words regretfully spoken in anger, words that should have been spoken but never were, unresolved conflicts, or the inability to say

final good-byes—these thoughts become the rich soil in which guilt and contempt thrive. In time, unresolved guilt tends to get channeled into either self-centered or other-centered contempt. Guilt exacts payment. Somebody will pay.

GUILT EXACTS PAYMENT. SOMEBODY WILL PAY.

I battled great guilt over not acting on a dream I had the night before Mom died. I wouldn't call it a premonition, but I do remember having some sort of feeling that something bad was going to happen to my mother. For years, I had no idea what to do with the sense of "Maybe I'm responsible for my mother's death. If only I had said something to her the next morning, perhaps I'd still have a mom." I did not become a Christian until seven years later, so I didn't really have a place to take my guilt. I had no lasting relief from this haunting "What if?" until I was convinced of the sovereignty of God and the gospel of his grace.

Loneliness. This is, perhaps, the most dangerous period in grief's seasons. What the heart does with loneliness largely determines the length of the journey toward healing. To get stuck here is to have relational patterns for the future significantly affected. For many, appropriate sadness leads to a battle with depression—a battle that can become a war. As the sadness intensifies, options to medicate the pain are multiplied, weighed, and chosen.

Our "drug of choice" may be one or more of the following: "rebound" relationships or disengaging from all relationships, drug and alcohol abuse, busyness and workaholism, hyperspiritualism—

and these are just a few of the many routes we can take in response to the pain of loneliness.

Rather than deal with my loneliness, I ran from the pain like a long-distance—make that a cross-country—track star. I simply added to my temple of idols as I continued the race. Not being a part of a healing community, I simply did the best an eleven-year-old could do. After my denial wore off, relationally I learned how to have associations without developing close friendships. It was safer that way. No one got my heart. This enabled me to minimize my pain and guarantee a certain amount of protection as I headed into the future.

In early teen years, I had my first exposure to pornography, and this "felt good" to a lonely heart; it was stimulation without the danger of relationship. Then sugar took over. Food became an idol, and I inherited—make that *earned*—the nickname "Meatball," a name I did not wear proudly. The television also took over in our home. I rarely remember it ever being off. Vicarious relationships with comedians, musicians, and adventurers provided distraction, but no real relief.

In high school, I learned how to find my way into "the popular circle," largely by losing forty pounds and obsessively spending every penny I could make on new clothes. As a freshman in high school, I looked at the "superlatives" given each year to members of the senior class and determined that I would set my goal on winning Best Dressed. (A noble goal, don't you think?) Mission accomplished. Talk about "fig leaves!" "Don't look at my heart; look at my clothes."

It was also in high school that I started to abuse alcohol, beginning

with cough medicine, then beer, and then grain alcohol. This was also the season in which I found my identity playing keyboards in a beach-music band that played mostly at colleges and universities up and down the East Coast. Performing on a stage became a way of life. It was so safe. Watch me, enjoy me, like me—but don't dare know me. Perhaps this is why I have yet to attend a single one of my high school reunions. I don't really miss anybody from those years.

When I became a Christian in 1968, my conversion was quite real. But I immediately headed in the direction of learning the content of the faith rather than the relational world of the faith. That Christianity was *true* meant more to me than that it was primarily about true *relationships*. I became an apologist and a teacher. I loved the writings of Francis Schaeffer and C. S. Lewis (although until recent years, I stayed away from *A Grief Observed,* the grueling account of how Lewis dealt with the death of his beloved wife, Joy).

When I became a member of the New Directions—a troupe of fifty young warriors singing together and doing evangelism—my penchant for performing onstage was fueled once again. I became a "leader" because of age and up-front gifts, not because of people skills. This is the same pattern I brought into the pastorate. Through the years, I have been far more comfortable in front of hundreds, even thousands, of people with a microphone in my hand than in a room full of strangers who have no idea who I am. Give me a crowd to teach over an angry, messy marriage to counsel any day. It's far safer!

Relief. The most intense pain of grief is transformed as we learn to access the comfort of God. Paul writes, "Praise be to the God and

Father of our Lord Jesus Christ, the Father of compassion and the God of all comfort, who comforts us in all our troubles" (2 Corinthians 1:3–4). God himself is committed to comforting us—in *all* "losses and crosses." This is won-derfully good news. But how does he do so? What are the means? Through his Word, by his gospel, through his people, by his Spirit—and all in his time. All of these are important, but each works best as we come to see

> THE VERY EVENTS THAT CAUSE US THE MOST PAIN IN LIFE CAN BECOME THE MEANS BY WHICH WE ARE EQUIPPED TO LOVE GOD AND OTHERS.

God's purpose in bringing us comfort. I remember Dan Allender once telling me, "Scotty, as long as your cry for relief is louder than your cry for a changed heart, you will remain a prisoner to your pain and a hostage of self-pity." Relief is more about freedom to love again than it is finally feeling good again.

Recovery. For Christians, the final stage of grief should not be thought of as "getting over" the pain as much as growing though it. The goal—always—is loving well. (Am I beginning to sound like a broken record?) God comforts us in all of our troubles "so that we can comfort those in any trouble with the comfort we ourselves have received from God" (2 Corinthians 1:4). We dare not waste our sor-rows on ourselves, and we dare not hoard God's comfort for ourselves.

The very events that cause us the most pain in life can become the means by which we are equipped to love God and others with a depth we would have otherwise never known. However, an unwill-ingness or failure to take this healing path can keep us strangers to God's affections and isolated in the world of relationships.

OBSTACLE #2: TOXIC FAITH EXPERIENCES

Abuse in any form can rob the heart of the joy of deep connecting, but religious abuse holds the power to distort our image of God and kill any desire or hope of being intimate with him.

I have a good friend whose late sixties' spiritual journey took him and his wife into a cultlike Christian group on the West Coast. Their newfound love for God was sabotaged, however, by the rigorism, control, and abuse of authority by the leaders in this group. Their childlike faith was also distorted by a heavy diet of teaching about the requirements of the law of God in the absence of clear teaching about his grace and the finished work of Jesus on the cross. After spending years in this fellowship and moving across the country with friends to be a part of a church plant, Bob and Mary began to question the autocratic and autonomous rule of the elders. This led to their expulsion from the group.

They found their way into our church family a few years later. Bob's longing but inability to worship God as a loving Father soon became obvious. He was far more comfortable talking about the ethics and principles of the Bible than he was in engaging in talk about knowing God with passion and delight. He was also extremely suspicious of those in authority in our church family, including myself. Though his heart told him otherwise, God was not a Father to be trusted and loved; he was a faceless deity to be feared and obeyed.

NOTHING HAS GREATER POWER TO ROB ANY OF US OF AN INTIMATE RELATIONSHIP WITH GOD THAN LEGALISM.

By exposing their hearts to what the Bible *really* says about God and his grace, Bob and his wife were healed from the toxicity of their religious abuse. He immersed himself in a study of two of the apostle Paul's letters, Galatians and Romans. In Galatians 4:15, he had a collision with Paul's question bitingly delivered to believers in Galatia, "What has happened to all your joy?"

The Galatian believers had also come under the influence of bad leaders and bad theology. The net result? The joy of knowing the full and free acceptance with God the Father through the finished work of Jesus was negated by legalism and legalistic leaders. Nothing has greater power to rob any of us of an intimate relationship with God than legalism—the damnable lie that our acceptance with God depends on something other than the finished work of Jesus Christ on our behalf.

I have had the joy of watching Bob and his wife come alive to the love of God, which is lavished on the ill-deserving through the gospel of his grace. Bob now serves as an elder in our church, and I know no man who walks more intimately and delightfully with the Father.

Such toxic faith experiences and religious abuse are not only found in cultlike groups like the one Bob and Mary came from. On one extreme, there are those who have experienced the horrors of satanic ritualistic abuse—yes, in communities like yours and mine. But also, in every denomination and nondenominational church in America, there are those who continue to live like joyless spiritual orphans rather than as beloved sons and daughters in whom our heavenly Father finds great delight. The reason? The toxic power of legalism.

OBSTACLE #3: MISPLACED AND DISSIPATED LOVE

What more could any one of us want in life and in death than to be able to say with assurance and joy, "I belong to my lover, and his desire is for me" (Song of Songs 7:10). To know this to be *our* relationship with Jesus and *his* with us is almost too much to fathom, yet it is the testimony of the Scriptures.

As we begin to see the Christian life revealed in the Bible as a "sacred romance," then our pursuit of other loves takes on the face of adultery, and our hearts are poised to see all sin as the battle for our heart's affections. To know oneself to be the beloved bride of Jesus Christ is to be in a position to grieve over the many ways we give our hearts to far lesser loves.

The apostle Paul describes the last phase of history in these terms: "There will be terrible times in the last days. People will be lovers of themselves, lovers of money…without love…not lovers of the good…lovers of pleasure rather than lovers of God" (2 Timothy 3:1–4). According to this scripture, the period between the two comings of Christ can be summarized as the tragedy of misplaced love. There is always something offering a greater attraction, a more satisfying promise, and a richer payoff than the love of God. Intimacy with God is assailed by whores, mistresses, and a whole host of one-night stands.

In my marriage it is very hard for Darlene to experience intimacy with me and me with her when my heart is preoccupied with other "lovers." Something is always competing with and waging war against our commitment to love and cherish one another above all other human relationships. I am sure that at times she feels as if she is married to a polygamist, a man who has several wives. One of those "wives" is named "job," another "ministry," another "sports," and still another "noise" (that's what she calls my loud music!). The truth is, when the finitude of my attention and passion is spread out among too many

> THE MORE WE LOVE GOD, THE LESS WE WILL LOVE OTHER GODS.

loves, I stop really enjoying Darlene. Intimacy in all of its dimensions goes south, real fast! As this is true in our marriages to our spouses, how much more so in our marriage to Jesus? So how can we come to freedom and focus in our relationship with God? How can we get free from spiritual polygamy?

Thomas Chalmers, a nineteenth-century Scottish pastor of great renown, once preached a penetrating sermon titled "The Expulsive Power of a New Affection." The premise of his word was simple but quite profound. The cathedral of the heart, he said, has only so much room. The best way to rid its chambers of unworthy loves is to cultivate a mighty affection for God himself. In other words, the more we love God, the less we will love other gods. But this requires intentionality and time—like any good relationship. We must learn to "romance" God through worship and by giving ourselves to the "means of grace"—that is, the means God has given us to grow in his grace—such as prayer, meditation on his Word, fellowship with other believers, and the Lord's Supper.

OBSTACLE #4: LIVING WITH DECEIT

Nothing so contaminates and destroys any sense of intimacy with my wife than when I live dishonestly with her. Secrets, hiddenness, or

an unwillingness to own my sin, failures, and foolishness causes her good heart to shut down in my presence as I continue my dance of pretense. Until I humble myself and live honestly with a gentled brokenness before her, I rob both of us of the richness of intimate connecting. But time and again, as I sincerely acknowledge my failure in love and openness, Darlene welcomes me into the embrace of grace. Why does it take my proud heart so long to get to brokenness?

As this pattern shows up in our marriages and friendships, how much more so in our relationship with God. King David proclaimed:

> Blessed is he
>> whose transgressions are forgiven,
>> whose sins are covered.
> Blessed is the man
>> whose sin the LORD does not count
>>> against him
>> and in whose spirit is no deceit.
> When I kept silent,
>> my bones wasted away
>> through my groaning all day long.
> For day and night
>> your hand was heavy upon me;
> my strength was sapped
>> as in the heat of summer.
> Then I acknowledged my sin to you
>> and did not cover up my iniquity.
> I said, "I will confess
>> my transgressions to the LORD"—
> and you forgave
>> the guilt of my sin. (Psalm 32:1–5)

David writes of the supreme joy of experiencing rich intimacy with God by his grace and the "bone wasting away" agony of living dishonestly before him. How foolish we are to hide from the One who longs to be gracious to us! When we confess our sins to God, we are informing him of nothing. The Greek word used in the New Testament for "confession" is *homologeo.* It means "to say the same thing as"—or in other words, to agree with what someone already knows to be true. God knows every bit of our stupidity, idolatry, and proclivity to wander from the One we love. That's why he sent Jesus!

Only as we live a life of confession and repentance before his throne of grace can we enjoy the intimacy for which we have been made. We rob both God and our own hearts of precious fellowship as we forestall coming home in our gentled brokenness to the Father who throws dance parties and feasts for his prodigal sons and daughters.

OBSTACLE #5: BUSYNESS

Several summers ago, my family had the privilege of visiting the great art museum in Paris called the Louvre. What an amazing collection of many of the world's most highly celebrated and priceless artifacts from centuries of craftsmanship. (By the way, I couldn't believe how small the *Mona Lisa* is.) While in Paris, a missionary friend told me that statistics from the curators at the Louvre show that the average American tourist takes only six seconds to drink in each piece of art—six measly seconds! What can anyone expect to absorb in only one-tenth of a minute?

I am told that deceased author and priest Henri Nouwen spent three whole days examining and studying every detail of Rembrandt's painting *Return of the Prodigal* before writing a book

on the parable of the prodigal son (Luke 15:11–32). The exquisite fruit of his quiet, unhurried study bleeds through every page of Nouwen's mature reflections. He wrote not as an art critic but as one who felt the Father's welcoming arms pressing his own broken heart into his warm breast.

A few years ago, I had to have arthroscopic surgery for a meniscus tear in my left knee. I've been jogging for about the past seventeen years. Finally, the price of not stretching, running on the wrong surfaces, and not changing shoes as often as I should had taken their toll. I hated it. It wasn't the surgery that I hated but the lack of mobility that resulted from it. For weeks I had to spend time sitting still, going to physical therapy once a week, and performing painfully slow rehab exercises. And worst of all, I was not able to run for a *long* time. The truth is, as I look back, I preached some of my best sermons during that season of stillness and weakness. I was forced to be at least physically still.

A desperately restless man is learning to be still and to know that God is God and that he is good. "It was good that I was afflicted of the Lord that I might learn to trust in him" (Psalm 119:71, paraphrased).

The direct correlation between how much time we spend studying, examining, meditating, and contemplating the beauty of Jesus and our experience of his love should be obvious.

It was obvious to the apostle Paul. Speaking of the wonderful freedom that we participants in the New Covenant community have, he affirmed, "And we, who with unveiled faces all reflect [as in *reflect upon* or *contemplate*] the Lord's glory, are being transformed into his likeness with ever-increasing glory, which comes from the Lord, who is the Spirit" (2 Corinthians 3:18). The more time we spend reflecting upon our Lord's glory, the more we will become like him.

OBSTACLE #6: INDIFFERENCE TO GOD'S PASSIONS

Why would any of us hope to enjoy an intimate and delightful relationship with God if we have very little regard for the things he is most passionate about? When I speak the three sweet words "I love you" to Darlene, she either laughs, gives me a playful hug, or returns my gaze with eyes brimming with love. Why? She knows the difference between the "I love you" that only means "I am looking for affection tonight," the "I love you" that means nothing more than "Hello, how ya doing?" and the "I love you" that tastes like "Tell me about your day, your dreams, your fears, feelings, and passions." Guess which one she likes the best?

ARE WE REALLY BEING INTIMATE WITH GOD, OR ARE WE SIMPLY ENJOYING A POWERFUL RELIGIOUS EXPERIENCE?

What are we really saying when we sing and pray, "I love you, Lord"? As we lift our hands and voices to the accompaniment of gifted worship leaders and great praise bands and choirs, are we really being intimate with God, or are we simply enjoying a powerful religious experience? Are we really passionate about God's passions and God himself?

God spoke to believers in the days of the prophet Amos:

I hate, I despise your religious feasts;
   I cannot stand your assemblies.
Even though you bring me burnt
      offerings and grain offerings,

I will not accept them.
Though you bring choice fellowship
          offerings,
    I will have no regard for them.
Away with the noise of your songs!
    I will not listen to the music of your
          harps.
But let justice roll on like a river,
    righteousness like a never-failing
          stream! (Amos 5:21–24)

Ouch!

Perhaps a contemporary paraphrase of this passage and similar words spoken by God through some of his other prophets would sound something like this: "I am wearied of your praise and worship services; quite frankly, I am bored with them. Your 'sacrifice of praise' requires little sacrifice and is empty of substantive praise. You are singing love songs—not to me, but to each other. You are enjoying yourselves a whole lot more than you are enjoying me, and I'm certainly not enjoying the whole thing very much!

"Do you want to make the kind of music that really thrills my heart? Would you like to give passionate meaning to your 'I love you, Lord'? Then give yourselves to working for justice in your communities. Take care of the poor and provide for the widows and orphans all around you. Love each other as I love you. Share the good news of my Son with the nations of the world. Work to push back the effects of the Fall wherever you can. Act justly in all situations. Love my mercy that I freely and gladly give you and extend it to all. Walk with me humbly all the days I give you in this world. As you live this way, it will sound like a mighty river of praise to me. It will be the greatest symphony I could ever hope to hear. Angels will marvel, and I will delight in such worship."

Would we develop intimacy with God that is more than lip service? Then let us learn to love and invest in his passions, which are the transforming of the world though his love and the harvest of his sons and daughters from among all the nations of the world. This is the true worship service.

OBSTACLE #7: UNBELIEF

Doesn't God tell us that we don't have because we don't ask? (James 4:3). Hasn't he told us that he can do immeasurably more than all we can ask or imagine? (Ephesians 3:20). Isn't he the God of the impossible? (Luke 1:37). I have a pretty well-documented track record of being a dullard and doofus when it comes to anticipating God's answers to prayer on my behalf.

I so identify with the believers who prayed for Peter's release from prison (Acts 12). As they cried out earnestly to God, there came a knock at the door—*Bam! Bam! Bam!* A young woman, Rhoda, heard Peter's voice, and in her excitement she told the others, "Peter is at the door!" They immediately responded, "You're out of your mind. It must be his angel." Now think about it. What would take more faith: believing that an angel was at the door or that Peter was there? I guess the thought of God actually answering their prayer was too much to take in!

Peter kept on knocking. It wasn't until they opened the door that they realized God had, indeed, answered their prayers. There

stood Peter, not his angel, bringing astonishment to everyone's heart. Are you in that crowd? That very house church? Have you prayed for years for God to do something in your life and then when he does, you can scarcely believe it? Then you are like me.

Let's bring that same principle and question to the issue of God's love for you. How can any of us expect to enjoy a rich and intimate relationship with God when we make him out to be a liar? As you ponder the staggering promises and declarations found in the Bible concerning the height, depth, width, and breadth of the love that God has for you in Christ, would you not agree with me that these words seem too good to be true? Yet the basis of our not experiencing the reality and richness of God's love is found either in God's dishonesty or in our unbelief. What do you think? Is God out-and-out lying, or are we simply not believing him? Let's pray together, "Lord, we believe; help us in our unbelief."

Perhaps the best way to finish our study together is to close with one more immersion in the river of God's affection as we take a glimpse at the life of the beloved ones. I dare you to believe what follows.

*G*od of Tender Affections,

That you have pursued relationship with me moves my heart to profound gratitude. That you actually call me to a growing intimacy with you moves me to awe and worship. Who am I, O Lord, that you should favor me with such rich communion? It is joy indeed to be able to say with confidence, "I am my Beloved's, and his desire is for me."

Forgive me for running into the arms of lesser loves. Why would I ever choose one-night stands with strangers over your abiding love and enduring affection?

It is a loving rebuke to my soul that you remember and miss the love I had for you at first. Your holy jealousy moves me to return and forsake my barren ways.

As I come, I welcome your fresh work in my heart, Jesus. Search me by the light of the gospel. Reveal to me the ways and reasons I resist you. When I prefer to do things *for* you, like Martha, rather than spend time *with* you, like Mary, convict the performer in me. When, like Peter, I refuse to let you wash my feet, arrest my pride.

Let me become as the woman who adoringly washed your feet with her salty tears. She loved much because you forgave her many sins. May such grace so capture my heart that I will cry out with fresh conviction, "Whom do I have in heaven but you, and earth has nothing I desire besides you." Through your holy name I pray, amen.

THEN I SAW A NEW *heaven* AND A NEW EARTH,
FOR THE FIRST *heaven* AND THE FIRST EARTH
HAD PASSED AWAY, AND THERE WAS NO LONGER ANY SEA.
I SAW THE HOLY CITY, THE NEW *Jerusalem,*
COMING DOWN OUT OF *heaven* FROM GOD,
PREPARED AS A BRIDE *beautifully* DRESSED
FOR HER HUSBAND.
—REVELATION 21:1–2

O how great Thy loving *kindness,*
vaster, broader than the sea!
O how *marvelous* Thy goodness lavished all on me!
Yes, I rest in Thee, Beloved,
know what wealth of grace is Thine,
Know Thy certainty of *promise,*
and have made it mine.
Jesus, I am resting, resting in the *joy* of what Thou art;
I am finding out the greatness of Thy loving heart.

*J*ean S. Pigot (1845–1882)

CHAPTER TEN

Life as the Beloved

Mary Jo stood out from all the other girls on the playground. She had strawberry blond hair, dimpled cheeks, and was awesome at kickball. I remember going to a movie with her on a Saturday morning when we were only seven years old. I shudder to call that my first date, but there we were.

Arriving at the (you guessed it) Graham Movie Theater a little late, we had to sit on the first row, which meant we had to look straight up at the screen. Sinking down in our seats to minimize neck pain, I remember the strange impulse I had about thirty minutes into the film to give Mary Jo a peck on the cheek. As young as we were, such a romantic notion had never before entered into my prehormonal system. Maybe it was the sentimental power of our movie that called forth the first stirrings of passion in my soul— *Bambi!*

I sat there plotting my move. Finally, in an irrational moment of unrestrained passion, I leaned in, gave her a little kiss on the left cheek—and took off running! Bolting for the back of the theater as though I had just committed grand theft, I calmed my beating heart, bought a box of Milk Duds to share with my first girlfriend, and returned to my seat as if nothing had happened.

On Monday of the next week we exchanged our first love letters:

I like you. Do you like me?

Check Yes _____ Check No _____

Not exactly the stuff that inspired Shakespeare to write *Romeo and Juliet,* but we were sincere. With the coyness of first-grader excitement, we grinned like possums when, during recess, we read the affirmations of each other's romantic inquiries. We were now officially "going together."

But tragedy struck early. By Wednesday, we "broke up." I caught Mary Jo talking to another boy during lunch. That was it! My jealous rage took over. What did she think I was, a fool? How could she play with my heart strings like that when I had already kissed her and we had eaten out of the same box of Milk Duds? So ended my first experience of romantic love.

HERE COMES THE BRIDE

As one who has performed hundreds of nuptial rites, I have often thought about writing a small booklet chronicling some of the more laughable, embarrassing, and touching wedding anecdotes I've witnessed during the past twenty-five years. Such a journal would sober young idealists planning their celebration and offer consolation to parents humiliated by some unforeseen faux pas. Whether wearing a robe in a cathedral, tuxedo in a chapel, denim in a backyard, or in my bare feet on the beach—I won't say that I have seen it all, but I've got a pretty good catalogue of "Yes, this can happen at *your* well-planned expensive wedding too" stories.

One such incident was what I call "The Tale of the Overly Expectant Groom." As the Maid of Honor arrived at her station just to my right, the last strand of Pachelbel's "Canon in D" faded to silence. During this well-orchestrated moment, I motioned to the elegant mother of the bride to stand and face the back of the sanctuary in honor of her daughter, soon to enter the vested gathering of family and friends. With all the stops pulled out, the organist sounded the first notes of the great hymn "Crown Him with Many Crowns," cuing the ushers to open two massive hand-carved oak doors.

There she stood, radiant with spring flowers woven into her flowing brunette tresses. Nothing could have prepared me for what happened next. No sooner did the bride take her first step through the doors than the groom left my side and started running up the aisle to meet his sweetheart. Hiking my robe a few inches, I took off after him and literally pulled him back by the arm. This spontaneous moment of unbridled affection proved to be more endearing than disruptive to our formal sensibilities.

I could tell you stories of humbling and humorous accounts of fainting groomsmen, wailing bridesmaids, *horrible* singers, flower girls who never made it up the aisle, and ring bearers who picked their noses and scratched themselves to the mortification of doting moms and grandmothers. Time does not allow me to expand on the

banner day when, during the solemnity of the exchanging of the vows, I called the groom by the name of the bride's *previous* boyfriend. Ouch. Come to think of it, I don't remember ever getting an honorarium for that one.

In a category altogether different from and more profound than anecdotes, there are those weddings I have performed which have served as epiphanies for me—moments of profound insight into what it means for us as Christians to be cherished and romanced by the only perfect groom and husband, Jesus. It has been in the middle of such ceremonies that I have experienced the presence of God and the incomprehensibility of his love surpassed by no other worship venue or liturgy.

God Makes All Things New

Fourteen-year-old Julie sat, staring at the floor at the entrance to the church office. She was about to become a charter member of my first youth group in Tennessee. I had just moved to Nashville to be the youth pastor at the First Presbyterian Church. Julie's mom, affectionately known as "Biddy," was our receptionist.

As I introduced myself to Julie, she had a hard time forcing herself to make eye contact with me. When she did look up, I realized why. Her jaws had only recently been wired shut to correct a severe misalignment. Julie's eyes revealed the physical and emotional pain any teenage girl would know experiencing such a trauma. Drinking your meals through a straw is one thing; having to endure the looks, the silence, and the limitations forced upon you as a teenager, so vulnerable in the journey of identity, is quite another.

Flash-forward with me to about a decade later. I stood with Scott, her fiancé, at my familiar post in front of the chancel area of our old and rather aesthetically unimpressive sanctuary. When the plain, ordinary uncarved doors opened and we all beheld Julie in her wedding gown, the room seemed to become like St. Paul's Cathedral in downtown London. Indeed, it *was* a royal wedding, for the Prince of Glory was present.

The sheer radiance of *this* bride did not make me want to run up the aisle like my unfettered friend; it made me want to fall down and worship Jesus who had utterly transformed this disheartened little girl into a woman overflowing as a fountain of God's grace and beauty. She was a testimony to the power of the compelling and consuming love of God, which is found nowhere but in the gospel. I wept tears of joy and worship as I tried to make it through each part of the service.

During the ten years I had known Julie, Jesus had been relentlessly pursuing her. Her high school years were not filled with enviable stories of a frenzied and full date life. Julie wasn't chosen to be the homecoming queen. Though well liked and loved by many, it would

SIPPING LIFE THROUGH A STRAW CANNOT COMPARE WITH DRINKING FREELY FROM THE ARTESIAN WELL OF ETERNAL LIFE THAT JESUS FREELY GIVES.

be during her college years at "Ole Miss" that the bud would give way to the bloom. I will never forget when I got word of her engagement. Surprise gave way to astonishment when I sat with Julie, whom I had not seen very much after her graduation from high school, and heard and saw the testimony of how she had come alive

to the love of God. The gospel of God's sovereign and passionate grace had literally transformed her.

She beamed poise, confidence, beauty, and peace—all evidence of what it can mean to rest in the embrace of the Lover of our souls. Though I have never had my jaws wired shut, Julie's transformation reminded me of how many years my heart has been wired shut—a stranger to the wild affections of our heavenly Bridegroom for his beloved. Sipping life through a straw cannot compare with drinking freely from the artesian well of eternal life that Jesus freely gives. On Scott and Julie's wedding day, I witnessed the power of God's love to make all things new and I heard the loud invitation to bring my thirst to Jesus.

STRONGER AFFECTIONS

If there were such a thing as an emotional intensity meter, and if I wore one every time I performed a marriage ceremony; then a graph of the last quarter of a century would reveal a definite pattern: The older I've gotten, the more pronounced my emotions have become—at least during the twenty-eight to forty-seven minutes it takes me to lead the worship service we call a marriage ceremony. Over the years, I've gone from near flat line to, at times, Pikes Peak on the emotional scale.

WEDDINGS ARE BECOMING FOR ME A DRAMATIC SYMBOL OF GRACE BY WHICH I EXPERIENCE THE MYSTERY AND MEASURE OF JESUS' LOVE FOR HIS BRIDE.

Why is this so? Two reasons come to mind. On one hand I have spent quite a bit of time meditating on the rich tapestry of scriptures that develops the central theme of a holy and passionate romance between God and his people. Second, I am coming alive to my longings to know this love firsthand. Therefore, weddings are becoming for me a dramatic symbol, a visual feast, a holy party; indeed, a means of grace by which I experience the mystery and measure of Jesus' love for his bride, including me.

A SINGING BRIDEGROOM

We turn once again to the prophet Zephaniah and the passage in which exquisite images and great truths tie together all the themes of this book. We read again—for its message makes us want to read it over and over again—"He will rejoice over you with singing"! (Zephaniah 3:17). What an awesome picture of the affection and joy that *Jesus* brings to his relationship with us.

> THE LORD HIMSELF BREAKS FORTH IN SONG AS HE CONTEMPLATES *US*, HIS CHERISHED PEOPLE.

To whom is the prophet referring in this magnificent montage? Who is doing the impassioned singing? Not an archangel, not one of the appointed soloists in the heavenly choir, not a favorite loved one who has already gone to heaven—but the Lord himself breaks forth in song as he contemplates *us*, his cherished people.

In a parallel passage that expands this magnificent metaphor of our singing God, the prophet Isaiah wrote of the outpouring of grace that would mark the Messianic age. "As a bridegroom rejoices over his bride, so will your God rejoice over you" (Isaiah 62:5). The singing God of Zephaniah's vision is the singing Savior of Isaiah—even Jesus, the Messiah, who emerges in the New Testament as the Savior-Bridegroom, the one who would rather die than live without

his beloved. Jesus is the fulfillment of this sacred romance, and he is taking a most unlikely bride for himself, you and me.

> JESUS WOULD RATHER DIE THAN LIVE WITHOUT HIS BELOVED.

As I try to imagine God rejoicing and singing over me as a part of the people of God, my natural instinct is to charge Zephaniah and Isaiah with prophetic exaggeration and poetic license. *Surely they are overstating the case to make a point. God doesn't sing, does he? And even if he does, certainly not when he considers me.*

What about you? Can you conceive of God serenading *you* with the passionate joy and committed tenderness of wedding-day bliss? If you are at all like me, then you struggle with a sense of being unworthy of such affection. Maybe God loves martyrs and missionaries in this fashion, but not me.

THE UNWORTHY BRIDE

Yet one of the main story lines of the Bible is that of God's taking an unworthy bride for himself. "For your Maker is your husband—the LORD Almighty is his name—the Holy One of Israel is your Redeemer; he is called the God of all the earth" (Isaiah 54:5). Most poignant of all is the way the book of Hosea communicates the scandalous romance between God and a disgraceful bride. To demonstrate the nature and eternality of his love for his people, God called Hosea to marry Gomer—most likely a prostitute who evidenced no intentions of leaving the "world's oldest profession" after the marriage.

From the depths of his own personal and domestic pain, the

prophet reveals the relentless compassion and all-conquering patience of our God, who was still very much in love with his unfaithful wife. Edward T. Welch eloquently tells the story:

> God was saying to Hosea, in effect, "You and I are both going to give our hearts completely to someone who will utterly reject us. We will give all of our hearts, energy, time, and money in pursuit of them. By doing this, you, Hosea, will understand my faithful love for you and your people. You see, I, myself, am the husband. Your life will be about my love. Your pain will point to my own. And your faithfulness will be a replica of mine."[1]

It didn't take long for Gomer to reveal her unfaithful, wandering heart. Her second child, a daughter, was named Lo-Ruhamah, which means "not loved," and her third child, Lo-Ammi, was a son whose Hebrew name means "not my people" (Hosea 1:6–9). In all likelihood, Hosea conceived neither of these children.

As with Hosea's wife so with God's people, Israel: Unfaithfulness abounded (Hosea 2:1–5). "She decked herself with rings and jewelry, and went after her lovers, but me she forgot" (Hosea 2:13). How would God the unrequited Lover and forgotten Husband respond to the adulteries of his own bride? Though justice would require otherwise, mercy and grace prevailed. God chose to pursue Israel, not to condemn her, but to caress her.

HOW WOULD GOD THE UNREQUITED LOVER RESPOND TO THE ADULTERIES OF HIS OWN BRIDE?

"Therefore I am going to allure her; I will lead her into the desert and speak tenderly to her" (Hosea 2:14). How could a desert be a place for stirring fresh affections? Sometimes God has to take us into a hard place in order to wean our hearts away from the illusions of

love in the city. "There I will give her back her vineyards, and will make the Valley of Achor a door of hope. There she will sing as in the days of her youth, as in the day she came up out of Egypt" (Hosea 2:15). God will replace the shame of a whore with the song of a virgin.

SOMETIMES GOD HAS TO TAKE US INTO A HARD PLACE IN ORDER TO WEAN OUR HEARTS AWAY FROM THE ILLUSIONS OF LOVE IN THE CITY.

"'In that day,' declares the LORD, 'you will call me "my husband"; you will no longer call me "my master."'... I will betroth you to me forever; I will betroth you in righteousness and justice, in love and compassion. I will betroth you in faithfulness, and you will acknowledge the Lord'" (Hosea 2:16, 19–20). Please notice all of the first-person, personal pronouns in these covenant promises. God alone can renew the heart.

Hosea was instructed to act out this same totally unexpected and unwarranted demonstration of unconditional love: "The LORD said to me, 'Go, show your love to your wife again, though she is loved by another and is an adulteress. Love her as the LORD loves the Israelites though they turn to other gods and love the sacred raisin cakes'" (Hosea 3:1). (Sacred raisin cakes represent food offered in the worship of the false god Baal.)

TO DIE FOR

By this time, Gomer's free-spirited ways had won for her a life of humiliating enslavement. The Scriptures teach there is pleasure in sin...for a season. But seasons change. Gomer eventually received the wages of her sin. But now, her true lover would offer the currency of mercy to redeem her out of slavery. Bought in the market-place for half the price of a common slave, Gomer's story is one of the clearest expressions of the gospel of God's grace found in the Old Testament. Wearing nothing but the nakedness of her shame, she is clothed in the goodness of another.

> THE SCRIPTURES TEACH THERE IS PLEASURE IN SIN... FOR A SEASON. BUT SEASONS CHANGE.

It took only six ounces of silver and ten bushels of barley to redeem Gomer. But the price God had to pay to lavish an idolatrous, adulterous people with his affection was much greater. Indeed, though his compassion was aroused to the point of not carrying out his justified "fierce anger" against Israel, his justice was not compromised; it was only withheld until the day when he came "in wrath" (Hosea 11:9).

In our case, however, the wrath was spilled out—not upon us, but upon his own Son. The Bridegroom, himself, became the condemned, naked slave of sin and death upon the cross. Because Jesus suffered in our place, we are now clothed with wedding garments of grace and righteousness.

> Bearing shame and scoffing rude,
> In my place condemned He stood,
> Sealed my pardon with His blood...
> Guilty vile and helpless we;
> Spotless Lamb of God was He.
> "Full atonement!" can it be?
> Hallelujah! what a Savior![2]

Greater love has no husband for his wife than to lay down his life for her. Greater love cannot be conceived than God dying for a thankless adulteress.

> GREATER LOVE CAN-
> NOT BE CONCEIVED
> THAN GOD DYING
> FOR A THANKLESS
> ADULTERESS.

It is *this* love that my spirit now feasts upon every time I officiate a wedding. When I see servantlike love in the eyes of a young groom, I am reminded of Jesus' matchless romance with his bride, the church. When I witness a "Romeo and Juliet" kind of love, I remember that while Romeo took his life because he could not be with his Juliet, Jesus laid down his life so that he will *always* be with his beloved. A beautiful bride's focused love and joyful willingness to "lay it all down" for her groom tantalizes us with a taste of the love from which all other loves derive their meaning.

GOD'S POEMS OF LOVE

As many thoughtful grooms and husbands write—or at least attempt to write—creative love poems and letters conveying their affection to their "darling," so God has written to us with the joyful and playful passion of a great lover. Consider the following words from The Song of Songs not merely as a picture of the provocative intimacy shared between a committed husband and wife, but also a picture of how Jesus romances us as his bride. With images that cause the weak to blush, our God speaks:

> How beautiful you are, my darling!
>   Oh, how beautiful!
>   Your eyes behind your veil are doves.
> Your hair is like a flock of goats

descending from Mount Gilead.
Your teeth are like a flock of sheep just
      shorn,
   coming up from the washing.
Each has its twin;
   not one of them is alone.
Your lips are like a scarlet ribbon;
   your mouth is lovely.
Your temples behind your veil
   are like the halves of a pomegranate.
Your neck is like the tower of David,
   built with elegance;
on it hang a thousand shields,
   all of them shields of warriors.
Your two breasts are like two fawns,
   like twin fawns of a gazelle
   that browse among the lilies.
Until the day breaks
   and the shadows flee,
I will go to the mountain of myrrh
   and to the hill of incense.
All beautiful you are, my darling;
   there is no flaw in you....

You have stolen my heart, my sister, my bride;
   you have stolen my heart
with one glance of your eyes....
How delightful is your love, my sister,
     my bride!
   How much more pleasing is your
     love than wine. (Song of Songs 4:1–7, 9–10)

All right, so Solomon's metaphors are different from yours and
mine: goatlike hair, sheepish teeth (with none missing!), and a tower

for a neck. Nevertheless, don't miss the point of the passage. God is unashamedly committed to wooing his already won people into a deeper, richer relationship with himself. For many of us, being "romantic" is the prelude to the wedding. For God, it continues throughout eternity!

> DO WE HAVE THE FAITH TO BELIEVE THAT WE HAVE ACTUALLY STOLEN JESUS' HEART?

Most women who meditate upon Song of Songs have their hearts come alive to the beauty of the passion and pursuit reflected in the heart of this lover. Here is a husband who knows his wife in the purest and most intimate sense of the word. With an eye for detail he ponders every possible way to communicate the depth of his affection and the honor he enjoys in calling this one "mine." This scripture reflects not only an involved husband but also a cherished bride. Thus, she can cry out with delight, "I belong to my lover, and his desire is for me" (Song of Songs 7:10).

CHERISH IS THE WORD I USE TO DESCRIBE

Dare we believe that Jesus cherishes us as much as the lover in the Song of Songs cherished his beloved? Do we have the faith to believe that we have actually stolen Jesus' heart and that in him we are already accepted as flawless, that he delights in *our* love? Can we accept the possibility that Jesus *desires* us? This is what the Spirit of God is committed to bringing home to every one of our hearts. This is that for which we have been made! Charles Wesley's understanding of the call of the beloved is revealed in his hymns through words we sometimes sing without feeling their impact on our hearts:

Jesus, Lover of my soul,
Let me to Thy bosom fly....
Thou, O Christ, art all I want;
More than all in Thee I find....
Thou of life the fountain art,
Freely let me take of Thee;
Spring Thou up within my heart,
Rise to all eternity.

A word to the brothers: Men, what stirs within your hearts as you read these words so full of emotion and relational intensity? Experiencing the sacred romance has nothing to do with discovering your "feminine side." We are not talking about temperament or personality types. The desires—which at times rage within your soul—for deep connection can be confusing and misplaced. While risking the danger of sounding stereotypical, we men often relegate such feelings to weakness or else we channel the passion to lesser loves—such as business, sports, or affairs of the heart, mind, and body.

But along with the sisters, we men will be never more alive than when we sing Jean Pigot's lyrics from a full and free heart:

Jesus, I am resting, resting in the joy of what Thou are art;
I am finding out the greatness of Thy loving heart.
Thou hast bid me gaze upon Thee, and Thy beauty fills my
    soul
For by Thy transforming power, Thou hast made me whole.
O how great Thy loving kindness, vaster, broader than the sea!
O how marvelous Thy goodness lavished all on me!
Yes, I rest in Thee, Beloved, know what wealth of grace is
    Thine,
Know Thy certainty of promise, and have made it mine.

Why would any one of us not make more time to ponder the way Jesus loves us? The lover of our soul is pursuing us. Oh that each of us could hear him say today in the gospel, "All beautiful you are, my darling; there is no flaw in you…. You have stolen my heart….

> JESUS, ALONE, HAS THE LOVE THAT CAN FILL US UP AND ENABLE US TO BE POURED OUT FOR OTHERS.

How delightful is your love." Then we could respond, "He has taken me to the banquet hall, and his banner over me is love" (Song of Songs 2:4). Jesus, alone, has the love that can fill us up and enable us to be poured out for others. There is no job, spouse, prostitute, friend, lover, or amount of money or achievement that can fill the ache of our souls. We are made for glory.

OUR SINGING SAVIOR

Do you remember when Bert and Ernie stood outside of Jimmy Stewart and Donna Reed's window serenading them on that cold, rainy honeymoon night, "I love you truly, truly I do…"? Captured in Frank Capra's much loved film *It's a Wonderful Life,* these two friends showered the much-loved newlyweds with the music of the heart. But as touching a scene as that is, how much more compelling is the revelation of Jesus serenading his own bride—even before the wedding feast begins. Jesus sings the music of eternal love in our midst and into our hearts. Where do we hear our Bridegroom sing the clearest and loudest?

Dr. Ed Clowney, former president of Westminster Theological Seminary, has given profound insight into the unfolding revelation of our Great Lover's singing.

In the New Testament, Jesus Christ comes as the Son of David, the sweet singer of Israel, to reveal God's love. In the upper room, Jesus sang with his disciples before he went out to the Garden of Gethsemane. On the cross, he uttered the opening cry of Psalm 22, "My God, my God, why have you forsaken me?" Hebrews attributes to Christ a later verse from that same psalm: "I will declare your name to my brothers; in the presence of the congregation I will sing your praises" (Hebrews 2:12; Psalm 22:22).

Jesus, who voiced the opening plea of dereliction, also utters the cry of triumph in the same psalm, and now sings in the midst of the congregation as he pays his vow of praise. Our triumphant King is a singing Savior. He sings with us here on earth and we with him in the assembly of heaven. Jesus is the heavenly Choirmaster, the Lord's anointed (2 Samuel 23:1). The apostle Paul applies to Christ the words of Psalm 18:49: "Therefore I will praise you among the Gentiles; I will sing hymns to your name" (Romans 15:9).[3]

What will it be like to hear Jesus sing in heaven? Let's enjoy just pondering the promise of that day. But for now, we can hear him sing most directly to us in the gospel. It is those who have abandoned all hope and every attempt to merit God's acceptance that hear most distinctly the joyful singing of Jesus over them. "I have loved you with an everlasting love; I have drawn you with lovingkindness" (Jeremiah 31:3).

And as the beloved bride, we sing back to our singing Bridegroom. In a context so rich with marital imagery regaling Christ's love for the church, Paul exhorts us to "Sing and make music in your heart to the Lord" (Ephesians 5:19). Consider the impact on our worship services if we saw ourselves joyfully singing back to the One who rejoices over us with singing.

The antiphonal singing between Jesus and his bride reminds me of one of the most unique weddings of which I have ever been a part. After nearly an hour of worship singing, a lengthy sermon from my co-officiant, and a groomsman passing out—the bride and the groom turned to one another and burst out in song. At that point *I* almost passed out!

CONSIDER THE IMPACT ON OUR WORSHIP SERVICES IF WE SAW OURSELVES JOYFULLY SINGING BACK TO THE ONE WHO REJOICES OVER US WITH SINGING.

Though I certainly did not sing to my wife at our wedding (for fear of being left at the altar), I now have a greater appreciation for the spontaneous, unabashed love this couple demonstrated to one another and shared so openly with the rest of us. Oh, that my proud heart were more poised and tuned to hear the enthusiastic singing of Jesus for me in the gospel! And I long to sing back to Jesus with the humbled astonishment that cries, "Out of all the world you have chosen me as your beloved!"

COVENANT SECURITY AND FIDELITY

As couples speak of covenant promise to each other, so Jesus has entered into an inviolate marriage covenant with us. Jeremiah received one of the most mind-boggling glimpses into the lavish love God promised his people through the work of the Messiah, Jesus:

> They will be my people, and I will be their God. I will give
> them singleness of heart and action, so that they will always
> fear me for their own good and the good of their children after
> them. I will make an everlasting covenant with them: *I will*
> *never stop doing good to them*, and I will inspire them to fear me,

so that they will never turn away from me. I will rejoice in doing them good and will assuredly plant them in this land with all my heart and soul. (Jeremiah 32:38–41, emphasis mine)

How can we begin to measure the dimension and security of such promises? God has covenanted to *never* stop doing good things to his people—*never!* And he has committed himself to doing so with great rejoicing! He will plant every member of his beloved bride in the land of inheritance—with all his heart and soul! What price tag can the heart of man place of such a standing in grace? All other gold is fool's gold compared to these unsearchable riches.

This new covenant—unlike any human covenant—depends completely on God's provision and faithfulness. All human covenants or contracts depend upon the fidelity of two parties. Any human marriage can be broken by unfaithfulness—not so God's covenant with us. He will never divorce us! That is why the predominant pronoun in all prophecies of the New Covenant is "I." Only God is capable of loving so unilaterally! Only he is bound to stay in a loving relationship with covenant breakers. Dare we hope that God does, indeed, relate to *us* like this?

Though Jeremiah does not use the metaphor of husband and wife in this passage, the fulfillment of these covenant promises comes to us through the one who has taken us to be his bride by the shedding of his blood. "Christ is the mediator of a new covenant, that those who are called may receive the promised eternal inheritance—now that he has died as a ransom to set them free from the sins committed under the first covenant" (Hebrews 9:15). Jesus "has appeared once for all at

the end of the ages to do away with sin by the sacrifice of himself. Just as man is destined to die once, and after that to face judgment, so Christ was sacrificed once to take away the sins of many people; and he will appear a second time, not to bear sin, but to bring salvation to those who are waiting for him" (Hebrews 9:26–28).

> WE HEAR JESUS SPEAK TO US IN FULL VIEW OF OUR INFIDELITY, "HOW CAN I GIVE YOU UP, EPHRAIM?"

Jesus has completely fulfilled the demands of the covenant, and he will never forsake his commitment to us. He has already suffered the punishment for the many ways we break our marriage covenant with him.

In a culture that increasingly treats marriage like a temporary way station—existing primarily for personal fulfillment—in a day when Christians are finding it easier and easier to divorce one another for all kinds of unbiblical reasons—in a day like this, we hear Jesus speak to us in full view of our infidelity, "How can I give you up, Ephraim? How can I hand you over, Israel?… For I am God, and not man—the Holy One among you" (Hosea 11:8–9).

Let's be honest: If you or I were Hosea, wouldn't we have left Gomer in her slavery to despair, die, and rot?

Because Jesus is God and not a mere man like us, he will never disown or divorce us. He will bring to completion the good work the Father has begun in us. "If we are faithless, he will remain faithful, for he cannot disown himself" (2 Timothy 2:13). Thus, we sing, "O love, that will not let me go, I rest my weary soul in Thee."

As his beloved and longing bride, we await Jesus' return. In that glorious last day, called from every nation, tribe, people, and language, we will stand before the throne of God with wedding garments washed "in the blood of the Lamb" (Revelation 7:14).

THE KISS OF HEAVEN

I always love saying these words to a newly married husband: "You may now kiss your bride for the first time as your wife." In a most profound way, Jesus expresses his affection and commitment to us through the means of grace.

It is our Episcopal brothers and sisters whose liturgical tradition first introduced me to the concept of seeing the Lord's Supper as the "kiss of heaven." So high is their regard for the table of the Lord, so developed is their understanding of the true meaning of the sacrament, and so deep is their commitment to safeguard its integrity, that they have applied this holy and tender description to what is conveyed as we "do this in remembrance of me."

In fact, one of the main words that the New Testament uses to describe worship, *proskenuein*, literally means "to move toward to kiss." As we worship around the table of the Lord, we exchange the kiss of covenant fidelity

> AS WE WORSHIP AROUND THE TABLE OF THE LORD, WE EXCHANGE THE KISS OF COVENANT FIDELITY AND AFFECTION WITH THE LOVER OF OUR SOULS.

and affection with the Lover of our souls. To "proclaim the Lord's death until he comes" (1 Corinthians 11:26) is to preach the gospel of his grace to our own hearts and to the watching world.

Every time we drink the cup and eat the bread of communion, we should remind ourselves that there is no greater love that a husband can have for his wife than to give himself up for her. This is exactly what

Jesus has done for us by giving his body, in life and in death, to secure us as his own. The only way our altogether holy, pure, and loving Bridegroom could marry himself to an unworthy bride like us is through the sacrifice of his own blood, "to present her to himself as a radiant church, without stain or wrinkle or any other blemish, but holy and blameless" (Ephesians 5:26–27). This is how much Jesus loves me and has loved his whole bride throughout history and around the world. Let us go and love as he loves us.

> WE MERIT NOTHING, BUT WE PROFIT CONSIDERABLY AS WE GIVE OURSELVES TO THE DISCIPLINES OF GRACE.

Therefore, to think of the Lord's Supper as the "kiss of heaven" is to remember and affirm that it is Jesus who is constantly pursuing and fueling our relationship with him. He is the initiator extraordinaire! We partake, not as those who long to be loved, but as those who are fully loved already. We remember Jesus' death upon the cross, not merely as a memorial, but that we may know his saving and loving power in the present moment of our season of betrothed waiting.

To forsake this meal and other "means of grace"—such as prayer, fellowship, service, and meditation on the Scriptures—is to starve our hearts of God's rich and necessary provision. We merit nothing, but we profit considerably as we give ourselves to the disciplines of grace.

We need his "kiss" every day, for our wandering hearts are too easily enticed by other and lesser loves. We share in his real presence *now* in light of the feast we shall enjoy forever *then*, when Jesus returns for us to consummate our relationship with him and to usher in the final and eternal state of marital bliss.

CHAPTER TEN: *Life as the Beloved*

A CELEBRATION BEYOND IMAGINATION

With rare exceptions (I have a few stories!), all wedding receptions are wonderful—whether celebrated in a ballroom, the basement of a church, or in a barn. But at their best, they only point to the quintessential marriage reception and celebration that we will share together when Jesus comes back for his bride.

In Revelation, the last book of the Bible, the apostle John offers a brief description of Jesus' return that pushes the imagination to cosmic realms. Our first day in the new heavens and the new earth is inaugurated with a party that almost exhausts an encyclopedia of metaphors to describe:

> Then I heard what sounded like a great multitude, like the roar of rushing waters and like loud peals of thunder, shouting: "Hallelujah!
> For our Lord God Almighty reigns.
> Let us rejoice and be glad
>   and give him glory!
> For the wedding of the Lamb has come,
>   and his bride has made herself ready.
> Fine linen, bright and clean,
>   was given her to wear."…
> Then the angel said to me, "Write: 'Blessed are those who are invited to the wedding supper of the Lamb!'" And he added, "These are the true words of God."
> At this I fell at his feet to worship him. But he said to me, "Do not do it!… Worship God!" (Revelation 19:6–10)

> Then I saw a new heaven and a new earth, for the first heaven and the first earth had passed away, and there was no longer any sea. I saw the Holy City, the new Jerusalem, coming down out of heaven from God, prepared as a bride beautifully dressed

for her husband. And I heard a loud voice from the throne saying, "Now the dwelling of God is with men, and he will live with them. They will be his people and God himself will be with them and be their God. He will wipe away every tear from their eyes. There will be no more death or mourning or crying or pain, for the old order of things has passed away."
He who was seated on the throne said, "I am making everything new!" (Revelation 21:1–5)

One of my favorite movies is *Father of the Bride*, which chronicles a father's (played by Steve Martin) comedic and touching journey in preparing to give away his only daughter in marriage. When it is determined that the family's backyard is to be the location for the reception, Franke, an eccentric wedding planner, transforms the neighborhood domicile into a garden of delights. For all the trouble, hard work, and expense involved, the party turned out to be an incredible celebration of joy and love.

But *that* gladness is merely a foretaste—a teaser, hint, an appetizer—for the party that awaits us as the bride of Christ. John describes the whole of heaven breaking out into thunderous shouts of "Hallelujah!" as Jesus receives his lovely and loved bride. In fact, the aging apostle himself was so moved by the promise and vision of the day that he fell down and started to worship the angel who merely delivered this grand vision!

The "wedding feast of the Lamb" will not be held in a transformed backyard but in an entirely remade universe—the Garden of Eden on steroids! Just try to imagine such beauty, order, and joy!

JUST ONE MORE INVITATION?

As I write these concluding words, it's springtime and my desk has a taller than usual stack of wedding invitations to which I need to politely respond. (I often get in trouble with Darlene for letting her know about invitations *after* the wedding!) The truth is, there is ultimately only one wedding invitation to which any one of us must give our fullest and timely attention.

Let's repeat John's words of passionate appeal: "Blessed are those who are invited to the wedding supper of the Lamb!" Have *you* responded to your invitation? It's more appropriate to think of this appeal as a subpoena to grace than a mere wedding invitation. For Jesus has done a whole lot more than merely offering us an amazing relationship with himself. He is seeking and securing a beloved bride to cherish and enjoy forever in the new heavens and new earth. He is seeking you!

Think back over the stories and truths we've shared together in the preceding chapters and think about your own life. How do Zephaniah's words, images, and declarations call you to respond to *your* wedding invitation from Jesus? The following response can be yours as you come alive to the compelling love of God:

> The Lord, the King of Israel—Jesus—is with me and for me. I do not need to fear anything—in life or in death. He greatly delights in me—not because of what I have done but simply because he has made me an object of his affection through his mighty salvation. He has and he continues to quiet my troubled and doubting heart with the strength and tenderness of his unconditional love. I actually hear him singing over me with

much joy as his beloved bride. I know these things to be wondrously true because, by dying for me on his cross, Jesus has taken away all the punishment I deserve for my sins. Therefore, I will sing, be glad and rejoice with all my heart! (Zephaniah 3:15–17, paraphrased)

The Spirit and the bride say, "Come!" And let him who hears say, "Come!" Whoever is thirsty, let him come, and whoever wishes, let him take the free gift of the water of life. (Revelation 22:17)

There's no need to return a prestamped response card to *this* wedding invitation. Just say "Yes!" and continue to say "Yes!" to Jesus' joyful proposal and incomparable provision. You will discover, or discover once again, that he is running up the aisle toward his second coming to welcome and romance you forever.

What are you waiting for?

The king there in His beauty Without a veil is seen
It were a well-spent journey Though sev'n deaths lay between
The Lamb with His fair army Doth on Mount Zion stand
And glory, glory dwelleth in Emmanuel's land.

O Christ, He is the fountain the deep sweet well of love
The streams on earth I've tasted More deep I'll drink above
There to an ocean fullness His mercy doth expand
And glory, glory dwelleth in Emmanuel's land.

The bride eyes not her garment But her dear bridegroom's face
I will not gaze at glory But on my King of grace.
Not at the crown He giveth but on His pierced hand
The Lamb is all the glory of Emmanuel's land.[4]

Glorious Bridegroom,

Could it be, could it really be that you are poised with great anticipation and joy to come for me? What wondrous love is this, that you, O perfect Son of God, should lavish such tender affection on me? I feel so unworthy of such astonishing love.

Yet you bid me look not to my own merit but to yours. You, my Beloved, have given me a wedding garment of grace. You have robed me in your righteousness. Taken from the brothel of the world, you have washed me, accepted me, and you now love me unconditionally—for you have fully met all the just conditions of the Father's righteousness.

Continue to heal my deafness to your joyful singing over me in the gospel. May your serenade of grace make all other love songs seem as noise to my soul.

I love you because you first loved me. I delight in you because you greatly delight in me. I enjoy you because you enjoy me with no qualification. I sing to you because you sing over me...without ceasing and without restraint.

As I anticipate the day of the great wedding feast, how do I love you best? What praise, what adoration, what service, what investment of heart and life will proclaim with unsullied voice and glad abandonment, "Behold the beauty and matchless love of Jesus! He alone is worthy of everything you have and are!" What, O Lord, is your language of affection? Loose my heart, loose my tongue, loose my possessions, loose my hands, loose my days.... Amen.

EPILOGUE

Thanks, Mom

Dear Mom,

I've been meaning to write you for quite some time. No, that's not really true. I've *needed* to write you for a very long time. This letter is way, way overdue.

As I sit here on the ground slowly running my fingers over each letter and number on your weathered grave marker, I feel a strange friendship with sadness and kinship with hope. Somehow, the two go together.

Mom, I miss you with a pain that threatens disintegration but at the same time invites healing. I only wish I had allowed myself to miss you sooner. I couldn't pay the price of remembering you then, I cannot afford to forget you now. Mom, you were ripped out of my life not by fate, but by fatality, and the tear has ragged edges still. When your body broke, my soul broke. The older I get, the more it

hurts, not the less. A part of me now comfortably says that's as it should be.

Mom, can you believe it? I'm fifty. Your baby is fifty. You were just barely thirty-eight when we brought you here on that gray October day. I am so sorry it has taken me so long to come back, I really am. And I'm sorry I never sent you flowers. Not that you know the difference, but I do, and those I have tried to love know. Staying away has taken its toll—on me and on them. But it's good to be here now. I say that with peace.

Ever since that incomplete morning, I have hated good-byes. Mainly because I never got to say good-bye to you before you left. That led to *this* incomplete mourning. But just how would an eleven-year-old boy say "so long" to his mom forever?

If I knew you were going to die, I would have thanked you for so many things you gave me. I thank you now. Mom, I loved your smile. It was one of the first hints I had that there is a God and that he is good. Finally, I am able to look at all the great pictures I have of you and enjoy your face without being ashamed of my own tears. By the way, Kristin (oh yeah, she's my daughter) painted a portrait of you for me for Father's Day. You're sitting on the rocks at Fort Fisher looking like a "babe." Mom, you were beautiful.

I am crying more now than those days when you used to hold me as a little guy and assure me that everything would be all right. Maybe it's just a huge backlog of heart water that has begged release for decades. Maybe I'm finally being gentled. Either way, Mom, your smile makes me ache for something I will never fully know in this world.

And thanks for your passion. I fed on it. Everyone who knew you talked about how *alive* you were, Mom. That makes your absence so much harder to accept. If you had been boring or predictable, I'd still have missed you, but it's like Dad said, when you died, the life went out of all three of us. Your energy, presence, and personality were infectious.

This sounds weird, but thanks also for your sticky rice, frozen green peas, and earthquake cake. Do you remember the time you made me a chocolate cake with icing so thick, heavy, and runny that all three layers crumbled under the stress? Mom, you weren't that much of a cook. But I miss sitting at a table with you no matter what you served up.

Thanks for loving music—even though I could never get into your Tennessee Ernie Ford hymns record or *South Pacific* or Dad singing anything. Your love for melody forced Moose to become the musician he is today, and it gave me a language with which to feel.

I thank you for the way you loved. Watching Granny and Granddaddy miss you after you died scared me. You loved them so well, and your silenced laughter and calls marked them until the day they saw you again. Everybody hated your death—at least selfishly—because you loved caring so much.

But nobody was more affected by the loss of your love and life than Dad. Mom, he completely shut down, and I understand why. I've been reading through a stack of love letters the two of you sent each other from the time you first started dating until Moose was born four years later. What a romance! He found in you what he found nowhere else. You really loved and enjoyed each other. Thanks.

Understanding Dad's loss has made it easier for me to deal with the huge voids and real needs he wasn't able to fill in my life. Mom, I've got some big holes in my heart, but Dad never intentionally failed or hurt me. He did everything he knew how to do. I never felt resented or a bother, just alone.

By the way, Mom, I have no idea what you guys in heaven actually know about the details in this part of God's dominion, but I'd love to think you are aware of how Dad and I are starting to connect. It's so encouraging. I love him, Mom.

I finally got up enough courage to ask him some questions about you, and, Mom, he has been giving me his heart, even his tears! By the way, what's this about a dentist who tried to win you away from Dad when he was at sea, and is it really true that you were the one who proposed marriage to him?

Mom, on the tape, Dad also included specific details about the day you died and stuff about your car wreck that I never knew. I am so sorry for what you went through.

I also thank you for Cherry Grove Beach, "clam-digger" shorts, for making me take the baseball I stole from Ben Franklin's back to Mrs. Dillahay, for Sego when I was chubby, for folding my underwear, and for ballroom dance lessons. It would have been great to dance with you at my wedding.

And, Mom, thanks for making me go to Mrs. Boland's house to learn the Children's Catechism when I was six. I didn't want to do it, I fought you on it; but many years later, God used those memorized words to awaken a spiritual quest. Maybe you *do* know about that story. If the angels rejoice when one of us comes to faith in Jesus, I don't think it's too much of a stretch to think you've been in the middle of that joy as well—especially the day God's grace captured me.

By the way, after I became a Christian, I finally unzipped your zipper Bible that I kept like a rabbit's foot in my headboard after your wreck. It was great to find certain verses in Romans under-lined. The ones you highlighted gave me a lot of assurance—about both of us. Thanks for pointing me beyond yourself even when you were the only savior I trusted in.

Regrets? Mom, I have a ton. I've done a lot of stupid things in life that you would have been ashamed of. I am even sorrier as I place you and those things in the same thought frame. I'd like to think if you had been here, I wouldn't have acted the fool quite so much. There was so much I could have learned from you, so many things I could have been protected from, so many ways I could have been better prepared to be a husband, dad, friend, and person. Even now I would love your wisdom and wit about all kinds of things.

But God has been both gracious and generous to me, Mom. He's not limited or thwarted by anything. I've had to learn and relearn that I need him a whole lot more than I need you. But you already know that much better than I do. He does redeem, doesn't he?

Anger? Not until recently. I was afraid of it. Mom, I think I am learning to be angry in a good way. I know I hate death more than ever, especially yours. Do I feel abandoned? Sometimes, intensely so. But my anger for death and my sense of abandonment pales when I think about Jesus, and what he endured to finally defeat death and

rob the grave of its victory. Mom, you and I were torn apart by death, but Jesus was torn by death so that we will one day be together forever.

But who am I to be telling *you* these things? I've only been to seminary. You've been to heaven!

Mom, I am so looking forward to being with you. I hate that you have never met Darlene, Scott, Kristin, or Matt. But you will, indeed you will.

Until then, I want to honor your memory. I want to learn even more about you than I have been able to find out in this past year. I'm going to read more of your letters, linger longer before your pictures, ask Dad and Moose, and anybody else I can, about your life and legacy. I'll not be afraid to grieve more if grieving will free me to love with the love of God.

But even more than I want to honor your memory, Mom, I want to honor Jesus. I don't think I can ever make Jesus proud of me as his own, for he already loves me perfectly. But I can choose to follow him wherever the demands and delights of his love lead. Thinking about you makes me want to know him better.

With great joy I so look forward to being with you—in God's timing.

Love,
Scotty

DISCUSSION QUESTIONS

CHAPTER ONE: *The Restlessness Begins*

1. Have you ever responded to a painful experience with numbness? Share that experience and why you think numbness was your response.

2. What events have shaped you relationally?

3. Do you ever "detach" from painful circumstances? What provokes you to detach?

4. Describe some times when you've submitted to the pursuing heart of God. What did he show you or teach you?

5. What adjectives currently define your inner life?

6. Has anyone become a concrete and treasured expression of God's love to you? Who? Why?

7. In reading this chapter, were you made aware of any issues of your heart that you have not faced and dealt with? Share what you are comfortable sharing.

8. When you are faced with a "seemingly shameful revelation" about yourself or your life, what do you do? How do you feel?

9. Who can you count on to lovingly challenge, question, or rebuke you? How do you respond when they try?

10. How do you respond to others who try to share with you the deep hurts of their heart? What have you learned from this chapter that can help you respond more helpfully?

CHAPTER TWO: *God's Great Delight*

1. Do you worry that if people really knew you they would reject you? What has confirmed or dispelled this fear?

2. What would it feel like in your heart to know that God not only accepts you but that he also richly enjoys you? What effect would such a viewpoint have on how you think about God, yourself, and others?

3. As a child, what was your first exposure to God?

4. How can God ravenously love a people who are naturally objects of his wrath, not objects of his affection? Why would God be angry with us in the first place?

5. Why doesn't God's righteousness demand that he be forgiving?

6. Think about this image: A flood of deserved punishment has given way to a flood of undeserved affection. What do you see? Where is Jesus in this picture? Where are you? How do you feel?

7. What are you trusting in besides Jesus to right your relationship with God?

8. Describe what it might feel like to be an object of his affection. How are you experiencing God's love in fresh ways?

9. How does the truth that God *wanted* to create you rather than needed to create you change your view of him? Of yourself?

10. Do your daily sinful behaviors interfere with God's delight of you? Is the propitiation of Jesus once and for all? Does it cover all?

Chapter Three: *Blind Men Seeing*

1. How has God weaned your wayward heart away from things that hold no ultimate satisfaction?

2. What are some causes of complacency in your life in the midst of journeying into the different dimensions of God's love?

3. Reflect on this phrase: To be "clothed with Christ" is to accept one's inability to change and find acceptance with God apart from outside help.

4. What part of your life is God "remodeling" right now?

5. In which areas of your life do you want to actively apply the truth that "we are already fully accepted by God and acceptable to him only on the basis of his gift of grace"?

6. Do you know anyone who is alive to God's love? How can you tell? How are they different? What draws you to them?

7. What distorted views of God's love might you have in your heart? What truth have you learned that can counteract that distortion?

8. Which do you prefer right now: the predictability of your blindness or the adventure of sight? What is fearful about sight? Where is God taking you out of your comfort zones?

9. What do you fear you'll see if God opens your eyes?

10. Are you ready to have the eyes of your heart enlightened? Why or why not?

Chapter Four: *The Power of Life and Death*

1. In what arenas in your life do you most sense the "fear of man"? How does this fear affect you?

2. Who, besides God, have you allowed to define who you are?

3. What source of "power" do you tend to "plug into"?

4. How would you describe the abundant life in John 10:10?

5. What do you think it means to seek first the kingdom of God in Matthew 6:33?

6. In your opinion, what is the difference between going to church and going to Christ?

7. How would you describe someone who is a "conduit" of God's mercy and grace versus a "container"?

8. How does the love of God in your life affect how you treat others? Do you pursue reconciliation in the midst of conflict?

9. Do you hold tightly a memory of painful words spoken to you? Why do you allow such words to speak louder than God speaks to you through his Word?

10. If you see yourself primarily as a leaky love tank, how will this affect your view of God and your relationship with him?

CHAPTER FIVE: *The Longings of a Thirsty Soul*

1. Though you are drawn to weakness because of its reality in your own life, you fear it as well. What is scary about weakness to you? What doors do you fear it will open in your life?

2. How can being thirsty for God be a gift from God?

3. What is it about sharing weakness that connects us? Why do we "naturally despise our weakness"?

4. God disciplines in love, for love, and with love. How does this differ from your own model of discipline either growing up or now?

5. How does the love of God translate into your life currently?

6. Has God ever worked in your life to show you the difference between "theoretical" weakness and the real thing? Share the experience and what you learned.

7. How can accepting your inability and weakness bring hope and freedom?

8. What worthless idols are you clinging to that forfeit a deeper experience of God's grace?

9. What are some of the thieves in your life that rob of your experience of the love of God, that hinder your ability and freedom to share it with others?

10. Can you identify any providential disruptions in your own life?

CHAPTER SIX: *The Severity of God's Mercy*

1. Do you really want to get well? What do you stand to gain by remaining sick? What do you stand to gain by being healed?

2. Describe the relationship between grief and freedom in your life.

3. Do you allow yourself to get angry? Why or why not? What is God's perspective on anger?

4. Think about the agony of Jesus as he wailed over the death of his friend Lazarus. How does this glimpse of emotion draw you to the person of Jesus?

5. What relationships in your life need repair? How can you begin?

6. Why is God determined to change your heart, not just your habits?

7. Share an example of God's "severe mercy" in your own life.

8. In what ways do you feel as if God is turning up the heat in your life? Where are you in the process of learning to thank him for hardships and suffering? What encourages you during times like these?

9. How does embracing God's love give you the courage to confront your own issues?

10. What emotional or spiritual "breaks" do you have in your past that never healed correctly and may need to be "rebroken"? How can you begin this process?

CHAPTER SEVEN: *Your Story of God's Love*

1. What progress have you made in merging Jesus' story and your own? How can you connect them more?

2. Have you ever had an experience—through a movie or otherwise—where you saw yourself reflected in someone else's story? What new insight did you gain? How have you put what you learned into practice?

3. What did Abraham Kuyper mean when he said that God can pay us no greater compliment than being jealous for our love?

4. How do you reconcile the two seemingly contradictory ideas from Lamentations 3: Though God brings grief, he will show you compassion? What examples of this have you experienced in your life?

5. How does your perceived condition affect your view of the salvation offered in Jesus?

6. What is God doing currently to get your attention? In what ways are you able to see his pursuing heart?

7. What "domino effects of grace" have you experienced in your life lately? Do you believe God is good enough and big enough to do the impossible in your life?

8. How does knowing your story in the context of God's bigger story make a difference?

9. What does it mean to move from a privatized faith to the largeheartedness of a life of mercy and generosity in all of your relationships?

10. Why is self-awareness vital to growing in the love of God and Christlikeness? How does remembering the significant events of your life benefit you?

CHAPTER EIGHT: The Love of Suffering

1. Have you ever been in a situation where the most appropriate response to another's pain was to listen rather than to give answers? Under what circumstances is this response appropriate?

2. How does seeing things from God's perspective help you better handle your pain and suffering?

3. From the reasons listed in this chapter regarding why God allows suffering, which have proven true in your life.

4. What does it mean to "endure hardship as discipline"? (Hebrews 12:7–11).

5. Why do suffering and love seem so incompatible? How does the cross speak to such a seeming disparity?

6. What "spiritual braces" might God be using in your life right now to shape you? How should you respond to his correction?

7. Have you ever blamed God for your suffering when really the suffering was a result of your own sin?

8. Looking through hindsight, what difficulties have you lived through that have served a greater good?

9. Why did Jesus stay on the cross when he had the power to come down? What would have happened if he had come down?

10. What difference would it have made in the way Job reacted to his pain if he'd known of the conversation between Satan and God? What difference can knowledge of spiritual warfare make in how you handle your own pain?

CHAPTER NINE: *Obstacles to Intimacy*

1. As you ponder the idea of an intimate relationship with God, what images come to mind? How would you describe intimacy with God?

2. Of the several obstacles to intimacy mentioned in this chapter, which ones represent challenges in your journey to know God's loving heart and tender affections?

3. What benefit is there in investing time and emotional energy to grieving your losses before the Lord?

4. What stories can you share of your travels on the healing path of grief? Are those wounds still in need of the liberating power of God's grace? Where do you tend to get stuck in the journey toward healing?

5. How is the Christian's grief different from that of nonbelievers?

6. Why is it important that you not define "doing well" for the grieving person?

7. What part does anger play in your grieving process?

8. How do you "medicate" your pain other than with God's love?

9. What other "loves" rival your love for God? How can you get them off the throne of your heart?

10. How can the very events that cause you so much pain be part of your avenue to greater love for God and others?

Chapter Ten: *Life as the Beloved*

1. How can a wedding be a form of worship?

2. After reading the scriptures in this chapter, how has your image of a wedding, bride, or bridegroom changed? Share your understanding of the Lord as your Husband.

3. What does the story of Hosea and Gomer teach you about the faithfulness of God's love versus the unfaithfulness of yours?

4. Why does God sometimes take you to a "desert," or a hard place?

5. Share about a time when you felt God's renewal in your heart.

6. How does knowing that Jesus is singing for you in the gospel affect your heart and life?

7. What difference does it make in your life to know that God is bound to stay in a loving relationship with you no matter what you do or don't do?

8. Think through the disciplines, or "means" of grace (i.e., prayer, fellowship, service, meditation). How are they profitable but not meritorious?

9. Do you believe that Jesus desires you? If so, how has that belief changed your life? If not, what hinders you from accepting his love?

10. What about the passages in Zephaniah 3 has impressed you the most and changed the way you think about yourself, God, and others?

NOTES

INTRODUCTION

1. Joseph Hart, "Come, Ye Sinners, Poor and Needy," 1759.

CHAPTER TWO

1. O. Palmer Robertson, *The Books of Nahum, Habakkuk, and Zephaniah* (Grand Rapids, Mich.: Eerdmans, 1990), 336.
2. Ibid., 340–41.

CHAPTER THREE

1. D. A. Carson, *The Difficult Doctrine of the Love of God* (Wheaton, Ill.: Crossway, 2000), 11.
2. Aurelius Augustine, *Confessions,* trans. R. S. Pine-Coffin (New York: Penguin Books, 1961), 177–178 (viii, 12).
3. Ibid., 178 (viii, 12).
4. Heiko A. Oberman, *Luther: Man Between God and the Devil,* trans. Eileen Walliser-Schwarzbart (New York: Doubleday, 1992, orig. 1982), 315.

5. Ibid.

6. As quoted in Charles W. Carter, ed., *A Contemporary Wesleyan Theology* (Grand Rapids: Zondervan, 1983), 344.

CHAPTER FOUR

1. C. S. Lewis, *The Weight of Glory* (New York: MacMillan, 1980), 1–2.

2. John Piper, *Desiring God* (Portland, Ore.: Multnomah, 1986), 14, emphasis mine.

3. John Piper, *The Pleasures of God* (Portland, Ore.: Multnomah, 1991), 10.

4. Edward T. Welch, *When People Are Big and God Is Small* (Phillipsburg, N. J.: P & R Publishers, 1997), 13, emphasis mine.

5. David Powilson, "Idols of the Heart and 'Vanity Fair,'" *The Journal of Biblical Counseling* 13, no. 2 (Winter 1995): 36.

CHAPTER FIVE

1. C. H. Spurgeon, *Treasury of David* (Nashville, Tenn.: Thomas Nelson, 1997), 523.

CHAPTER SIX

1. Dan Allender, *Cry of the Soul* (Colorado Springs: Navpress and Tremper Longman III, 1994), 74.

CHAPTER TEN

1. Welch, *When People Are Big and God Is Small*, 173.

2. Phillip P. Bliss, "Hallelujah! What a Savior," 1875.

3. Ed Clowney, *The Church* (Downers Grove, Ill.: InterVarsity, 1995), 134–35.

4. Anne Cousin, "The Sands of Time Are Sinking," 1857.